YOUR LUNCHBOX

Bring Your Healthy Kitchen to the Office.

100+ Delightful Easy Recipes for Lunches

Silver
Edition

CONTENTS

—

'You are what you eat', a saying that resonates with profound truth. Our health, our vitality, even the brilliance of our thinking are influenced by the quality of the food we consume. Diet plays a crucial role not only in the prevention of many chronic diseases, but is a powerful ally for enjoying a full, energetic and extraordinarily vibrant life.

In our fast-paced society, the workplace often becomes a battleground between efficiency and well-being. One struggles to maintain concentration, to manage stress, to sustain the relentless pace of a working day. This is where lunch comes in, not only as a necessary break, but as a fundamental tool to ensure our well-being and performance.

Think of a meal at work as tailor-made: it reflects your uniqueness, your nutritional needs, your tastes.It's not just about calories, it's about nutrition.A well-balanced meal is a tailor-made suit that you wear every day: it dresses you with energy, makes you feel your best, helps you live to the fullest.

The art of a healthy and satisfying meal lies in the perfect balance of nutrients: carbohydrates, proteins and healthy fats. But the proportions of these ingredients can vary depending on many factors, from age, gender, body weight, health and physical activity. If you have any particular health conditions, food intolerances or allergies, always remember to consult a professional.

This is where the lunchbox, our everyday heroine, comes in.

This dialect word, rooted in our traditions, symbolises the perfect way to take a full, healthy meal with you wherever you are: office, school, university.It is your personal response to a hectic world, a daily reminder that taking care of yourself is possible, even amidst the hustle and bustle of modern life.The lunchbox is more than just a container for carrying and eating food. It is a declaration of independence, health and well-being. And in the course of these pages, you will discover how delicious, varied and surprising it can be.

Each recipe in this book is a journey to better health, a more balanced and tastier life. Dedicate yourself, discover the art of schlepping and embrace the joy of a healthy, nutritious and delicious lunch every day. Whether you are a worker, a student, an executive, you will find your perfect lunch in these pages. Eating healthy has never been easier or more delicious. And now, let's get ready to slip on the apron and bring the magic to life."

THE IDEAL CONTAINER FOR YOUR SCHISCETTA

Choosing the right container for your lunchbox is just as important as choosing the right recipes. Different materials and designs offer a variety of advantages, which can suit your specific needs. Here is a list of options to consider:

1. Plastic: Plastic containers, especially those made of polypropylene, are lightweight, impact-resistant and generally inexpensive. Many of them are designed to be used in the microwave, making them ideal for dishes such as reheatable pasta or rice. Make sure they are free of BPA (Bisphenol A), a potentially harmful organic compound.
2. Glass: Glass containers, usually borosilicate, are temperature-resistant, hygienic and do not absorb odours or colours from food. Ideal for salads, soups or stews, they can be used in the microwave and dishwasher. Glass, however, is heavier and more fragile than other materials.
3. Stainless steel: This material is extremely durable, easy to clean and safe for food storage. Perfect for cold food such as salads or sandwiches, it is, however, not suitable for use in the microwave. We recommend choosing a steel container marked 18/8 or 18/10.
4. Bamboo or wood: Bamboo or wood containers are environmentally friendly and add a natural and chic touch to your meal. They are not suitable for moist foods such as soups, and cannot be used in the microwave or dishwasher.
5. Silicone: Silicone containers are flexible, lightweight and durable. They can be used in the microwave, oven, refrigerator and dishwasher. In addition, many can be folded when not in use to save space. They are perfect for foods such as rice, pasta or salads.

As far as container types are concerned, there are many to choose from, each with its own advantages:

6. Containers with compartments: These containers have separate compartments that allow different foods to be separated, preventing them from mixing. They are perfect for balanced meals that include a variety of foods.
7. Thermal containers: These containers are designed to keep food hot or cold for several hours. They are ideal for meals that must be eaten at a certain temperature.
8. Bento box: These Japanese containers have separate compartments and are often used to create visually attractive meals. They are suitable for those who want a balanced and delicious meal.
9. Foldable containers: These containers save space when not in use, making them ideal for transport. They are especially useful if space in your bag or backpack is limited.
10. Leak-proof containers: These containers have airtight lids that prevent liquid or semi-liquid food from leaking out. They are perfect for soups, sauces or salads.

CLIMATE CHANGE AND OUR CULINARY CHOICES: TOWARDS A SUSTAINABLE FUTURE

Climate change manifests itself in our daily lives with palpable urgency. The limits of the earth's resources are undeniable, and the echoes of these changes echo in every aspect of our lives. Soon, we will face realities such as the rising cost of food and the displacement of entire populations from areas rendered unlivable by climate change.

However, at the heart of this turmoil, there is one aspect of our daily routine that holds extraordinary potential: our diet and the decisions we make at the supermarket. The reality is that every food we cook, every product we select, leaves a mark on our ecosystem.

While the food industry is a source of problems, it also represents an opportunity for change. Although it poses a serious threat to the Earth's biodiversity, it is also the ground on which we can begin to sow solutions. Research shows that a sustainable food regime can not only limit greenhouse gas emissions, but also enhance our ecosystem and increase our quality of life.

In the comfort of our homes, every wasted food represents an unnecessary consumption of resources, water and energy. The wasteful attitude, common in developed nations, exacerbates the erosion of our habitat. The zero-waste approach, increasingly popular among those adopting a careful lifestyle, encourages us to value every food product. What we usually discard can be transformed into the centrepiece of creative and tasty dishes. The zero-waste ethic motivates us to avoid excess, optimise what we own, recycle carefully and convert organic waste into valuable compost.

Our commitment goes beyond the moment of payment at the till: by opting for paper or reusable bags, we fight disposability; by choosing organic products, we promote sustainable farming methods; by getting organised, we can make use of every product we buy, turning leftovers into succulent dishes for days to come. Proper post-meal waste management and converting waste back into compost are manifestations of our respect for the planet. If we end up with extra food, let us donate it: it is a benefit to those who receive it and a demonstration of respect for the Earth.

Every decision made within the home brings us closer to a more prosperous and eco-friendly tomorrow. In an era of urgent climate crisis, our kitchen becomes a bastion of resilience, innovation and optimism.

FOOD WASTE, HIDDEN TREASURES

Reusing food waste has several advantages. Not only does it save money and combat food waste, but it can also offer significant nutritional benefits.
Let us look at some examples:

1. **Potato peels:** They contain a good amount of vitamin C, vitamin B6, potassium and fibre. They can be roasted in the oven with a little oil and salt to create crispy snacks or used in cleaning due to their degreasing properties.
2. **Herb stems:** The stems of parsley, coriander, basil, etc., contain many of the same vitamins and minerals as the leaves, including vitamin C, vitamin K and iron. They can be used to enrich broths and soups.
3. **Peels of citrus fruits:** The peels of lemons, oranges and limes are rich in vitamin C and contain bioactive compounds such as pectin and flavonoids, which have antioxidant properties. They can be used to make candied fruit, herbal teas or grated into recipes to add flavour.
4. **Outer leaves of vegetables:** The outer leaves of cabbage, lettuce, chard and other vegetables are rich in vitamins, minerals and fibre. They can be used to make soups, broths or stews.
5. **Pumpkin and melon seeds:** Pumpkin and melon seeds are rich in protein, fibre, magnesium and zinc. They can be roasted and used as a snack or as a topping for salads and soups.
6. **Apple cores:** Apple cores contain a good amount of fibre and vitamin C. They can be used to make apple broth or cider.
7. **Leek Tops:** Beneficial as the heart of the leek. Freeze them for broths, soups, sauces or use them fresh in wraps, sautéed vegetables, salads and pies.
8. **Celery leaves:** Celery leaves are rich in vitamin A, vitamin C and calcium. They can be used in salads, soups or as a garnish.
9. **Broccoli and cauliflower stems:** Often discarded, broccoli and cauliflower stems contain a good amount of vitamin C and fibre. They can be grated to make raw salads, or steamed, or used in soups and stews.
10. **Onion peels:** Although inedible, onion peels can be used to add flavour to broths. In addition, they contain phytochemical compounds that have antioxidant properties.
11. **Asparagus:** The end of the stalk is suitable for soups, broths and dressings. The cooking water is a nutritional concentrate, ideal for cooking pasta, rice or preparing detox herbal teas.
12. **Aubergine peels:** Aubergine peels contain a good amount of anthocyanins, a powerful antioxidant. They can be used in sauces, soups or stews.
13. **Celery leaves:** They offer similar benefits to ribs. They are aromatic and add flavour to broths, soups, sauces, pies, omelettes and are ideal for extracts and centrifuges.
14. **Cucumber peels:** Cucumber peels contain a good amount of vitamin K. They can be used in salads or as a garnish.
15. **Fruit and vegetable scraps from juicing:** After extracting the juice from fruit and vegetables, the scraps can be used to make crackers, muffins or incorporated into recipes for salads, soups and stews. They are rich in fibre and still contain a good amount of vitamins and minerals.

16. **Fennel Beard:** In addition to having carminative properties, it is excellent for depurative herbal teas, sauces, risottos, pestos, dressings, creams and soups.
17. **Pea pods:** Versatile for velvety soups, risottos, meatballs, casseroles, pestos, creams and dressings.
18. Artichoke Stems: Tender, they are ideal for pestos, creams, meatballs, burgers and fillings.
19. **Cabbage stalks:** Although tough, they are excellent in broths, velvety soups and soups enriched with rice or pasta.
20. **Turnip leaves:** Turnip leaves are rich in vitamins A, K and C, as well as calcium and iron. They can be steamed, sautéed or added to soups and stews.
21. **Fennel leaves:** Fennel leaves are rich in vitamins A, C and K, and can be used to enrich salads, soups or used as an aromatic herb in various recipes.
22. **Beetroot leaves:** Beetroot leaves contain a good amount of vitamins A, C and K as well as iron and calcium. They can be used in salads, soups or sautéed like spinach.
23. **Radish leaves:** Rich in pungent flavour that mellows with cooking, they are versatile for salads, omelettes, risottos, soups and pestos, or even stir-fried.
24. **Broad bean husks:** A source of dietary fibre, these husks fight constipation. Ideal for stir-fries, pesto, chips, creams, soups.
25. **Carrot Clumps:** Slightly bitter, but nutritious. Eat them raw in salads, sautéed, steamed or in omelettes, risottos, hummus, soups, meatballs and burgers.
26. **Carrot peels:** Once dried, they are excellent for broths, sauces, sautéed vegetables, chips, omelettes, pestos, vegetable burgers, hummus, savoury pies and flans.
27. **Broccoli Leaves and Stems:** The stems are perfect for cutlets, stir fry dishes, creams and pestos, while the leaves lend themselves to pasta, wraps, soups, meatballs, omelettes and savoury pies.

SPRING

SPRING SALAD OF SPELLED, ASPARAGUS AND PEAS

Preparation time: 20 min
Cooking time: 25 min

Calories:	400 kcal	Protein:	55 g
Fats:	15 g	Carbohydrates:	8 g
Fibres:	10 g	Sugars:	5 g

Ingredients

- 200g of spelt
- 300g of asparagus
- 2 handfuls of fresh peas
- 100g of Roman pecorino cheese
- Olive oil, salt and pepper q.b.

Preparation

1. Cooking spelt: Cook spelt in boiling salted water according to the instructions on the package. Once cooked, drain and let cool.
2. Preparation of asparagus: Clean the asparagus by removing the woody parts, cut them into pieces and steam them until they are tender but still crunchy.
3. Cooking the peas: Steam the fresh peas until tender.
4. Salad assembly: In a large bowl, combine cooled spelt, cooked asparagus, fresh peas and flaked pecorino cheese. Season with olive oil, salt and pepper to taste.
5. Preparation for transport: Transfer the salad to an airtight container and keep in the fridge until lunch.

NOTE 1 (pg 127)

02. COLD PASTA WITH CHERRY TOMATOES, ROCKET AND RICOTTA

Preparation time: 15 min
Cooking time: 10 min

Calories: 450 kcal   Protein: 65 g
Fats: 15 g   Carbohydrates: 8 g
Fibres: 10 g   Sugars: 5 g

Ingredients

- 200g of whole grain pasta
- 300g of cherry tomatoes
- 2 handfuls of arugula
- 200g of ricotta
- Olive oil, salt and pepper q.b.

Preparation

1. Cooking the pasta: Cook the pasta in salted boiling water according to the instructions on the package. Once cooked, drain and cool under cold water.
2. Preparing the tomatoes: Wash the tomatoes, cut them in half or in quarters.
3. Assembly of cold pasta: In a large bowl, combine the cooled pasta, cherry tomatoes, arugula and ricotta into small pieces. Season with olive oil, salt and pepper to taste.
4. Preparation for transport: Transfer the pasta to an airtight container and keep in the fridge until lunch.

03. SPRING QUINOA, CARROT AND COURGETTE OMELETTE

Preparation time: 15min
Cooking time: 15min

Calories: 400kcal   Protein: 45g
Fats: 20g   Carbohydrates: 8g
Fibres: 10g   Sugars: 5g

Ingredients

- 150g of quinoa
- 300g of carrots
- 300g of courgettes
- 4 eggs
- Olive oil, salt and pepper q.b.

Preparation

1. Cooking quinoa: Cook quinoa in salted boiling water according to the instructions on the package. Once cooked, drain and let cool.
2. Preparation of carrots and zucchini: Clean the carrots and zucchini and cut them into slices. Steam them until they are tender but still crunchy.
3. Preparation of the omelette: In a non-stick pan, pour a little oil and add the quinoa, carrots and zucchini. In a separate bowl, beat the eggs and pour over the quinoa and vegetables. Cook until the omelette is well done.
4. Preparation for transport: Transfer the omelet to an airtight container and keep in the fridge until lunch.

04. BULGUR WITH CHICKPEAS, CABBAGE AND PECORINO

Preparation time: 20 min
Cooking time: 30 min

Calories: 400 kcal   Protein: 50 g
Fats: 15 g   Carbohydrates: 10 g
Fibres: 10 g   Sugars: 5 g

Ingredients

- 200g of bulgur
- 200g of pre-cooked chickpeas
- 300g of cabbage
- 100g of pecorino cheese
- Olive oil, salt and pepper q.b.

Preparation

1. Cooking the bulgur: Cook the bulgur in salted boiling water according to the instructions on the package. Once cooked, drain it and let it cool.
2. Preparation of the cabbage: Clean the cabbage and cut it into thin strips. Steam until it is tender but still crunchy.
3. Dish assembly: In a large bowl, combine the cooled bulgur, chickpeas, cabbage and pecorino cheese flakes. Season with olive oil, salt and pepper to taste.
4. Preparation for transport: Transfer the bulgur with chickpeas and cabbage to an airtight container and refrigerate until lunch.

05. COUSCOUS WITH ASPARAGUS, TOMATOES AND BUFFALO MOZZARELLA

Preparation time: 15 min
Cooking time: 5 min

Calories: 400 kcal Protein: 50 g
Fats: 15 g Carbohydrates: 5 g
Fibres: 10 g Sugars: 5 g

Ingredients

- 200g of couscous
- 300g of asparagus
- 200g of cherry to-matoes
- 150g of buffalo moz-zarella cheese
- Olive oil, salt and pepper q.b.

Preparation

1. Preparing the couscous: Prepare the couscous according to the instructions on the package. Once ready, let it cool.
2. Cooking the asparagus: Clean the asparagus by removing the final part of the stem and steam them until they are not tender but still crunchy.
3. Preparation of tomatoes and mozzarella: Wash the tomatoes and cut them in half. Cut the mozzarella into cubes.
4. Dish assembly: In a bowl, combine couscous, asparagus, cherry tomatoes and mozzarella. Season with olive oil, salt and pepper to taste.
5. Preparation for transport: Transfer the couscous to an airtight container and keep in the fridge until lunch.

06. SPRING OMELETTE WITH ASPARAGUS AND CHIVES

Preparation time:	10 min	Calories:	200 kcal	Protein:	4 g
Cooking time:	12 min	Fats:	12 g	Carbohydrates:	2 g
		Fibres:	14 g	Sugars:	1 g

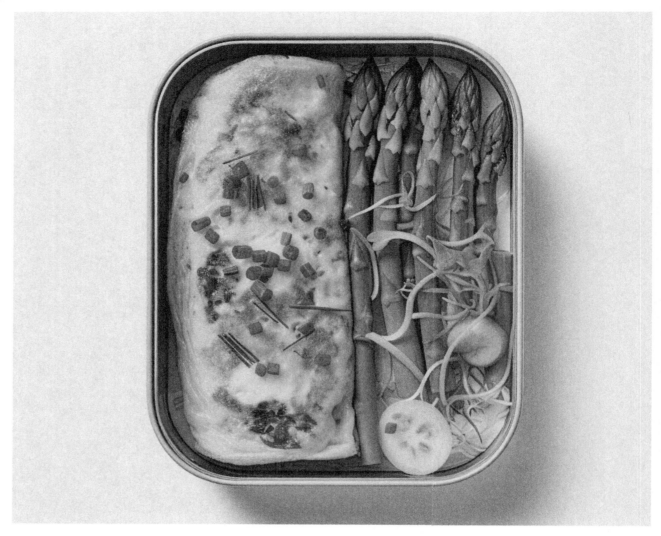

Ingredients

- 5 large eggs
- 150g of asparagus
- 2 tablespoons of chopped chives
- Salt and pepper q.b.
- 2 tablespoons of olive oil

Preparation

1. Asparagus preparation: Clean the asparagus by removing the hard end of the stem. Cut the asparagus into segments of about 3 cm.
2. Sauté the asparagus: In a non-stick pan, heat the olive oil and fry the asparagus for about 5 minutes until they become slightly tender.
3. Preparation of the eggs: In a bowl, beat the eggs with chives, salt and pepper until you get a homogeneous mixture.
4. Cooking the omelette: Pour the beaten eggs into the pan with the asparagus. Cook over medium-low heat, without stirring, for about 5-7 minutes or until the omelette is almost completely cooked but still soft in the center. Turn the omelet upside down and cook for another 2 minutes.
5. Preparation for transport: Transfer the omelet to an airtight container and keep in the fridge until lunch.

CRISPY SALAD OF ARTICHOKES, RADISHES AND ONIONS

Preparation time: 15 min
Cooking time: 0 min

Calories: 80 kcal   Protein: 8 g
Fats: 3 g   Carbohydrates: 5 g
Fibres: 4 g   Sugars: 2 g

Ingredients

- 2 fresh artichokes
- 5 radishes
- 2 spring onions
- Olive oil, salt and pepper q.b.
- Lemon juice q.b.

Preparation

1. Preparation of artichokes: Clean artichokes by removing the hard outer leaves and cutting the tips. Slice the heart of the artichoke thinly and put it in a bowl with water and lemon juice to prevent it from oxidizing.
2. Cutting radishes and spring onions: Wash and slice the radishes thinly. Clean and cut the spring onions into thin rings.
3. Salad assembly: In a large bowl, mix together artichokes, radishes and spring onions. Season with olive oil, salt, pepper and a pinch of lemon juice.
4. Preparation for transport: Transfer the salad to an airtight container and keep in the fridge until lunch.

08. RISOTTO WITH FRESH PEAS AND MINT

Preparation time: 20 min
Cooking time: 18 min

Calories: 370 kcal   Protein: 60 g
Fats: 11 g   Carbohydrates: 3 g
Fibres: 7 g   Sugars: 3 g

Ingredients

- 300g of Carnaroli or Arborio rice
- 250g of fresh peas, shelled
- 1 small chopped white onion
- 1 liter of vegetable broth
- 50g of grated Parmesan cheese
- A bunch of fresh mint chopped
- Olive oil, salt and pepper q.b.

Preparation

1. Preparation of the sauté: In a large pan, fry the chopped onion in olive oil until it becomes translucent, but not golden.
2. Rice cooking: Add the rice to the pan and toast for about 2 minutes, stirring well to make it flavor.
3. Adding peas and broth: Combine the fresh peas and cover with the hot vegetable broth. Stir well and cook over medium heat, adding the broth one ladle at a time every time the rice absorbs it.
4. Finish: After about 15-18 minutes, when the rice is al dente, remove from the heat and add the Parmigiano Reggiano and minced mint. Mix well and season with salt and pepper to taste.
5. Preparation for transport: Transfer the risotto to an airtight container and keep in the fridge until lunch.

SPAGHETTI WITH STRAWBERRIES AND ARUGULA

Preparation time:	10 min		
Cooking time:	10 min		

Calories:	350 kcal	Protein:	55 g
Fats:	12 g	Carbohydrates:	3 g
Fibres:	6 g	Sugars:	5 g

Ingredients

- 250g of spaghetti
- 200g of fresh straw-berries
- 100g of arugula
- 50g of grated par-mesan cheese
- Extra virgin olive oil, salt and pepper q.b.

Preparation

1. Cooking spaghetti: Cook the spaghetti in a pot of boiling salted water following the instructions on the package until it reaches an al dente consistency.
2. Preparing the strawberries: Clean and cut the strawberries into small pieces.
3. Dish assembly: Drain the spaghetti and transfer them to a bowl. Add strawberries, chopped arugula and season with olive oil, salt and pepper.
4. Finishing: Mix everything gently and garnish with grated parmesan cheese.
5. Preparation for transport: Transfer the spaghetti to an airtight container and keep in the fridge until lunch.

10. SPINACH QUICHE AND FETA CHEESE

Preparation time: 15 min
Cooking time: 35 min

Calories: 300 kcal Protein: 20 g
Fats: 10 g Carbohydrates: 2 g
Fibres: 20 g Sugars: 2 g

Ingredients

- 200g of fresh spinach
- 100g of feta cheese
- 3 eggs
- 1 roll of ready pastry
- 200 ml of kitchen cream
- Salt, pepper and nutmeg q.b.
- Olive oil q.b.

Preparation

1. Preparation of the base: Spread the pastry in a previously greased quiche pan, prick it with a fork and put it in the fridge for about 10 minutes.
2. Blanching of spinach: Rinse the spinach and dip in salted boiling water for 2 minutes. Drain and squeeze well to remove excess water.
3. Composition of the filling: In a bowl, beat the eggs with cream, add salt, pepper and a grated nutmeg. Combine the crumbled feta and spinach and mix well.
4. Filling and cooking: Pour the mixture on the basis of brisée dough. Bake in a preheated oven at 180 °C for 30-35 minutes or until the surface becomes golden.
5. Preparation for transport: Once cooled, transfer the quiche to an airtight container and refrigerate until lunch.

11. BEET WRAPS WITH FAVA BEANS AND AGRETTI

Preparation time: 20 min
Cooking time: 10 min

Calories: 150 kcal   Protein: 20 g
Fats: 7 g   Carbohydrates: 4 g
Fibres: 5 g   Sugars: 2 g

Ingredients

- 4 large leaves of chard
- 200g of fresh shelled broad beans
- 100g of clean crops
- Olive oil, salt and pepper q.b.

Preparation

1. Preparation of broad beans: Cook the beans in boiling salted water for 5 minutes, then drain and let cool.
2. Preparation of the agretti: Cook the agretti in salted boiling water for 3-4 minutes. Drain and let cool.
3. Wraps assembly: Lay the beet leaves on a worktop. Distribute the broad beans and agretti in the center of each leaf, season with olive oil, salt and pepper.
4. Wraps wrapping: Wrap the beet leaves around the filling, forming well-sealed wraps.
5. Preparation for transport: Transfer the wraps to an airtight container and store in the fridge until lunch.

12. LETTUCE AND RED TURNIP MEATBALLS

Preparation time: 15 min
Cooking time: 20 min

Calories: 220 kcal   Protein: 25 g
Fats: 8 g   Carbohydrates: 5 g
Fibres: 9 g   Sugars: 8 g

Ingredients

- 150g of fresh chopped lettuce
- 200g of cooked and chopped red turnips
- 50g of breadcrumbs
- 1 egg
- 2 tablespoons grated Parmesan cheese
- Olive oil, salt and pepper q.b.

Preparation

1. Preparation of vegetables: Wash lettuce and turnips thoroughly. Chop lettuce and red turnips into fine pieces.
2. Composition of the dough: In a bowl, combine the chopped lettuce and red turnips with egg, breadcrumbs, and grated parmesan. Mix well until you get a smooth dough and season with salt and pepper.
3. Meatball formation: Take a little dough at a time and form small meatballs, pressing well in your hands.
4. Cooking the meatballs: In a frying pan, heat a little olive oil and cook the meatballs for about 10 minutes, turning them often until they are golden and crunchy outside.
5. Preparation for transport: Once cooled, transfer the meatballs to an airtight container and refrigerate until lunch.

13. BRUSCHETTE WITH RAMERINO AND RICOTTA

Preparation time: 10 min
Cooking time: 5 min

Calories: 260 kcal
Fats: 10 g
Fibres: 12 g

Protein: 30 g
Carbohydrates: 4 g
Sugars: 3 g

Ingredients

- 4 slices of whole-meal bread
- 200g of fresh ricotta cheese
- 2 tablespoons chopped ramerino (rosemary)
- Olive oil, salt and pepper q.b.

Preparation

1. Toast the bread: In a grill or toaster, toast the slices of bread until they become crispy and golden brown.
2. Preparation of the ricotta: In a bowl, mix the ricotta with the chopped ramerino. Season with salt and pepper to taste.
3. Assembly of bruschetta: Spread generously the mixture of ricotta and twig on slices of toast. Season with olive oil.
4. Preparation for transport: Transfer the bruschetta in an airtight container, avoiding overlapping them, and keep in the fridge until lunch.

NOTE 13 (pg 127)

14. CHERRY AND TUNA TARTARE

Preparation time: 10 min
Cooking time: 0 min

Calories: 220 kcal   Protein: 8 g
Fats: 25 g   Carbohydrates: 1 g
Fibres: 8 g   Sugars: 7 g

Ingredients

- 150g of fresh tuna
- 100g fresh cherries, pitted
- 2 tablespoons chopped red onion
- 1 tablespoon extra virgin olive oil
- Salt and pepper q.b.
- Fresh basil leaves q.b. to garnish

Preparation

1. Preparation of tuna: Clean the fresh tuna by removing any bones or dark parts. Cut it into small cubes and uniform.
2. Preparation of cherries: After pitting, cut the cherries into small pieces.
3. Mixing the tartare: Combine the tuna cubes, cherries and chopped red onion in a bowl. Season with olive oil, salt and pepper. Stir gently until you get a smooth consistency.
4. Serving: Using a pastry ring, place the tartar on the plate and press lightly to give it a cylindrical shape. Remove the ring gently.
5. Garnish and transport: Garnish with fresh basil leaves. Transfer the tartar to an airtight container and refrigerate until lunch.

15. RHUBARB COLD SOUP AND TURNIP TOPS

Preparation time: 10min
Cooking time: 20min

Calories: 110kcal Protein: 15g
Fats: 3g Carbohydrates: 4g
Fibres: 4g Sugars: 3g

Ingredients

- 200g of rhubarb
- 150g of turnip greens
- 500ml of vegetable broth
- 1 tablespoon extra virgin olive oil
- Salt and pepper q.b.
- Natural yogurt q.b. for garnish

Preparation

1. Preparing the rhubarb: Clean and cut the rhubarb into pieces of about 2 cm.
2. Cooking turnip tops: Clean turnip tops and cook in salted boiling water for 10 minutes. Once cooked, drain and cool quickly under running water.
3. Cooking rhubarb: In a pot, bring the vegetable broth to a boil. Add the rhubarb pieces and cook for about 10 minutes or until tender.
4. Blending and seasoning: With the help of an immersion blender, blend the rhubarb and turnip greens together to a smooth cream. Season with olive oil, salt and pepper.
5. Cooling and transport: Let the soup cool completely, then transfer to an airtight container and refrigerate until lunch. When serving, garnish with a tablespoon of natural yogurt.

16. SAVORY ARTICHOKE CAKE, ZUCCHINI AND ZUCCHINI FLOWERS

Preparation time: 20 min
Cooking time: 35 min

Calories: 350 kcal   Protein: 30 g
Fats: 10 g   Carbohydrates: 6 g
Fibres: 20 g   Sugars: 4 g

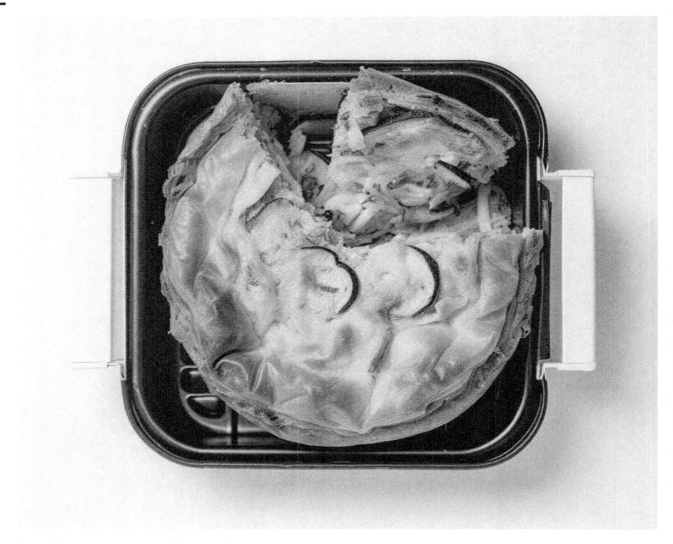

Ingredients

- Artichokes (3 medium)
- Zucchini (2 medium)
- Zucchini flowers (5-7 pieces)
- Spring onions (2, finely chopped)
- Eggs (4)
- Puff pastry or brisée (1 roll)
- Twig (2 twigs, finely chopped leaves)
- Olive oil, salt and pepper q.b.

Preparation

1. Cleaning Artichokes and Zucchini: Remove hard leaves and artichoke tips, divide, eliminate stubble and immerse in water with lemon. Wash the zucchini, cut them and clean the flowers by removing the pistil.
2. Sauté and Cook: In a pan with oil, fry onions and rosemary for 2 minutes. Add artichokes and zucchini and cook over medium heat for about 10-15 minutes, stirring occasionally, until tender. Add salt and pepper to taste.
3. Dough: Beat the eggs in a bowl, combine cooked vegetables and mix well. Make sure to evenly distribute the ingredients.
4. Pasta and Baking: Spread the dough in a baking sheet, bucherella, decorate with flowers. Pour the dough and cook at 180 ºC for 20-25 minutes, or until the surface is golden brown and the omelette is well cooked inside.
5. Cool and Preserve: Once cooked, let the pie cool for at least 10 minutes. Transfer it to an airtight container once completely cooled.

17. CRESSONELLA AND BEETROOT ROLLS

Preparation time: 10 min
Cooking time: 0 min

Calories: 300 kcal   Protein: 40 g
Fats: 10 g   Carbohydrates: 6 g
Fibres: 12 g   Sugars: 5 g

Ingredients

- 2 whole grain rolls
- 100g of cressonella (watercress)
- 1 beet cooked and sliced
- 50g of crumbled feta cheese
- Olive oil, salt and pepper q.b.

Preparation

1. Preparation of cressonella: Wash and dry the cressonella.
2. Bun assembly: Open whole grain buns and evenly distribute the cressonella, beet slices and feta cheese.
3. Seasoning: Pour a little olive oil on the rolls, add salt and pepper to taste.
4. Preparation for transport: Close the sandwiches and wrap them in baking paper or aluminium. Store in an airtight container or in a cooler until lunch.

18. CHICKEN ROLLS WITH PUNTARELLE AND BASIL

Preparation time: 15 min
Cooking time: 25 min

Calories: 220 kcal Protein: 3 g
Fats: 30 g Carbohydrates: 1 g
Fibres: 7 g Sugars: 1 g

Ingredients

- 2 chicken breasts
- 100g of puntarelle
- 10 leaves of basil
- 2 tablespoons of olive oil
- Salt and pepper q.b.

Preparation

1. Preparing the Puntarelle: Clean the puntarelle removing any hard or damaged parts and cut them into thin strips.
2. Chicken marinade: Cut the chicken breasts into thin horizontal strips and season with salt, pepper and a tablespoon of olive oil. Leave to marinate for 10 minutes.
3. Chicken Cooking: Heat a non-stick pan with a tablespoon of olive oil. Once warm, add the chicken strips and cook on both sides until they are well browned, about 10-12 minutes.
4. Roll assembly: On the cutting board, lay a strip of chicken, place a few strips of puntarelle and a basil leaf in the center. Wrap the chicken around the ingredients, forming a roll.
5. Preparation for transport: Transfer the rolls to an airtight container and keep in the fridge until lunch.

19. OMELETTE WITH BROCCOLI AND AIOLI

Preparation time:	10 min		
Cooking time:	15 min		

Calories:	280 kcal	Protein:	5 g
Fats:	18 g	Carbohydrates:	2 g
Fibres:	20 g	Sugars:	2 g

Ingredients

- 3 eggs
- 100g of broccoli
- 2 tablespoons aioli (garlic mayonnaise)
- 1 tablespoon of olive oil
- Salt and pepper q.b.

Preparation

1. Preparation of Broccoli: Clean the broccoli and cut them into small flowers. Steam for 5-7 minutes or until tender but still crunchy.
2. Preparation of the Omelette: In a bowl, beat the eggs with salt, pepper and a tablespoon of aioli until you get a homogeneous mixture.
3. Cooking the Omelette: Heat a non-stick pan with olive oil. Pour in the egg mixture and add the steamed broccoli. Cook the omelet for about 5-7 minutes or until it is well done, turning it once.
4. Finish: Once cooked, spread the omelet with the remaining aioli.
5. Preparation for transport: Fold it in half and transfer to an airtight container. Keep in the fridge until lunch.

20. BASKETS OF CHICKEN WITH ARTICHOKES AND BASIL

Preparation time: 10 min
Cooking time: 20 min

Calories: 260 kcal   Protein: 8 g
Fats: 30 g   Carbohydrates: 3 g
Fibres: 10 g   Sugars: 1 g

Ingredients

- 2 chicken breasts (about 300g)
- 150g artichoke hearts (already cleaned)
- 10 leaves of fresh basil
- 2 tablespoons of olive oil
- Salt and pepper q.b.

Preparation

1. Cooking the chicken: In a pan, heat a tablespoon of olive oil. Add chicken breasts, salali and pepali, and cook for 10 minutes on each side over medium heat, or until they become golden brown and well cooked inside. Once ready, transfer to a plate and let them cool.
2. Preparation of artichokes: In a separate pan, heat a tablespoon of oil and add the artichoke hearts. Cook over medium heat for 10 minutes or until tender. Add salt and pepper to taste.
3. Assembling the baskets: Finely chop the chilled chicken and drain with the artichokes in a pan. Cook together for 2-3 minutes. Turn off the heat and add the chopped basil leaves.
4. Preparation for transport: Transfer the mixture into airtight containers, ready to be taken to work.

21. ROLLS OF ASPARAGUS AND HAM

Preparation time: 10 min
Cooking time: 15 min

Calories: 220 kcal   Protein: 5 g
Fats: 14 g   Carbohydrates: 2 g
Fibres: 16 g   Sugars: 2 g

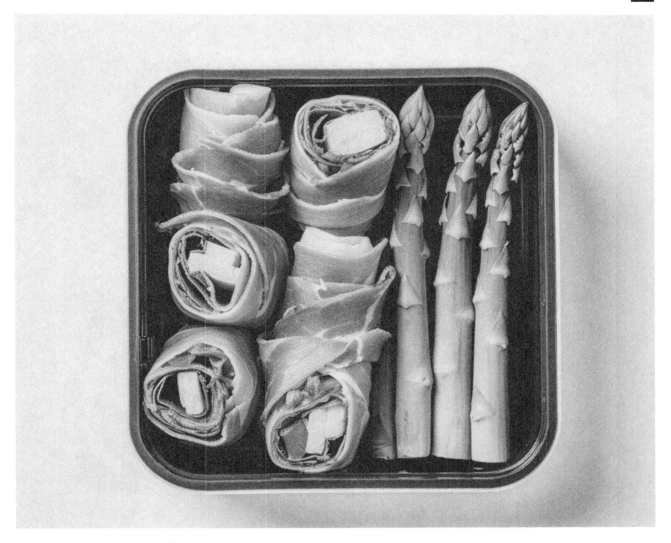

Ingredients

- 200g of couscous
- 300g of asparagus
- 2 tablespoons of capers
- Juice of 1 lemon
- Olive oil, salt and pepper q.b.

Preparation

1. Preparation of asparagus: Remove the hard end of the stem of asparagus and rinse under running water.
2. Cooking the asparagus: In a pan with a tablespoon of oil, cook the asparagus for 7-8 minutes, turning them occasionally, until they become tender but still crunchy.
3. Wrapping: Once cooked, wrap each asparagus with a slice of raw ham.
4. Finishing and cooking: Heat a non-stick pan and cook the rolls for 2-3 minutes per side, until the ham becomes crispy.
5. Preparation for transport: Transfer the rolls to an airtight container, ready to be taken to work.

NOTE 21 (pg 128)

22. SALT CREPES WITH BEANS AND CHIVES

| Preparation time: | 20 min |
| Cooking time: | 15 min |

Calories:	300 kcal	Protein:	45 g
Fats:	12 g	Carbohydrates:	5 g
Fibres:	8 g	Sugars:	5 g

Ingredients

- 150g of flour 00
- 250ml of milk
- 2 eggs
- 200g of fresh broad beans
- 30g of chopped chives
- 50g of grated parmesan cheese
- Olive oil, salt and pepper q.b.

Preparation

1. Preparation of the batter: In a bowl, mix the flour with the eggs, gradually add the milk and continue to mix until you get a smooth and homogeneous batter. Add a pinch of salt and let stand for 10 minutes.
2. Baking the crepes: Heat a non-stick pan lightly greased with oil. Pour a ladle of batter, distributing it evenly. Cook for about 2 minutes on each side or until golden brown. Repeat with all batter.
3. Preparation of broad beans: Boil the beans in boiling water for 5 minutes, then drain and let cool. Remove the outer skin.
4. Assembly of crepes: On the surface of each crepe, distribute the beans and chives. Sprinkle with grated parmesan and fold in half.
5. Preparation for transport: Transfer the crepes to an airtight container and keep in the fridge until lunch.

23. TORTINO DI PISELLI AND RICOTTA

Preparation time: 15min
Cooking time: 25min

Calories: 250kcal   Protein: 20g
Fats: 15g   Carbohydrates: 5g
Fibres: 10g   Sugars: 4g

Ingredients

- 300g of frozen peas
- 200g of ricotta
- 2 eggs
- 50g of grated parmesan cheese
- Salt, pepper and nutmeg q.b.
- Olive oil for greasing

Preparation

1. Cooking the peas: In a pot, boil the peas in salted boiling water for 7-8 minutes or until tender. Drain and let cool.
2. Preparation of the mixture: In a bowl, combine the ricotta, eggs and parmesan. Add peas, a pinch of salt, pepper and nutmeg to taste. Mix well.
3. Baking the cake: Preheat the oven to 180C. Oil a baking dish and pour the mixture inside, leveling with a spatula. Bake for 20 minutes or until the surface is golden brown and the center is cooked.
4. Rest and remove from the oven: Let the cake cool for at least 5 minutes before removing it.
5. Preparation for transport: Cut the cake into portions and transfer to an airtight container. Keep in the fridge until lunch.

24. FRESH MINT AND STRAWBERRY GAZPACHO

Preparation time: 20 min
Cooking time: 0 min

Calories: 150 kcal Protein: 20 g
Fats: 2 g Carbohydrates: 4 g
Fibres: 7 g Sugars: 13 g

Ingredients

- 400g of ripe strawberries
- 10 leaves of fresh mint
- 1 small cucumber
- 1 red pepper
- 1 clove of garlic
- Juice of 1 lemon
- 2 tablespoons extra virgin olive oil
- Salt and pepper q.b.

Preparation

1. Preparing the strawberries: Wash the strawberries under running water, remove the stalk and cut them in half.
2. Preparation of cucumber and bell pepper: Wash cucumber and bell pepper. Peel cucumber and remove seeds, then cut into cubes. Cut the pepper in half, remove the seeds and cut into pieces.
3. Ingredients processing: In a blender, combine strawberries, cucumber, bell pepper, peeled garlic clove, mint leaves, lemon juice, olive oil, salt and pepper. Blend until smooth and smooth.
4. Cooling: Transfer the gazpacho to a container and put it in the refrigerator for at least 2 hours before serving.
5. Preparation for transport: Transfer the Gazpacho to an airtight container and keep in the fridge until lunch.

25. CHICKEN SKEWERS AND MARINATED RADISHES

Preparation time:	30 min		
Cooking time:	15 min		

Calories:	350 kcal	Protein:	4 g
Fats:	35 g	Carbohydrates:	2 g
Fibres:	18 g	Sugars:	2 g

Ingredients

- 400g of chicken breast
- 200g of radishes
- Juice of 2 lemons
- 3 tablespoons extra virgin olive oil
- 1 tablespoon of dried oregano
- Salt and pepper q.b.

Preparation

1. Preparation of the chicken: Cut the chicken breast into cubes of about 2 cm.
2. Marinating the chicken: In a bowl, mix the lemon juice, olive oil, oregano, salt and pepper. Add the chicken cubes and mix well. Leave to marinate in the fridge for at least 30 minutes.
3. Preparing radishes: Wash the radishes and cut them in half.
4. Assembly of skewers: Insert alternately a piece of marinated chicken and half a radish on sticks for skewers.
5. Cooking the skewers: Pre-heat a grill or a non-stick pan over medium-high heat. Sew the skewers for about 6-7 minutes per side, or until the chicken is cooked and has a slight browning.
6. Preparation for transport: Once cooled, transfer the skewers in an airtight container and keep in the fridge until lunch.

—

SUMMER

01. WRAP OF TURKEY AND AVOCADO

Preparation time:	15 min		Calories:	400 kcal	Protein:	30 g
Cooking time:	0 min		Fats:	25 g	Carbohydrates:	10 g
			Fibres:	20 g	Sugars:	3 g

Ingredients

- 4 whole grain tor-tillas
- 200g of sliced tur-key breast
- 2 ripe avocados
- 4 leaves of lettuce
- Juice of 1 lemon
- Salt and pepper q.b.

Preparation

1. Avocado preparation: Cut the avocados in half, remove the core and crush the pulp with a fork until you get a cream.
2. Wrap assembly: Lay out a tortilla and spread with avocado cream. Add a lettuce leaf and place some turkey slices on top. Season with lemon juice, salt and pepper.
3. Wrap Closure: Roll up the tortilla on itself, trying to hold the ingredients tightly inside. Cut the wrap in half before serving.

02. QUINOA AND BEAN SALAD

Preparation time: 15 min
Cooking time: 15 min

Calories: 400 kcal
Fats: 15 g
Fibres: 10 g
Protein: 60 g
Carbohydrates: 10 g
Sugars: 5 g

Ingredients

- 200 grams of quinoa
- 400 grams of canned red beans
- 2 yellow peppers
- 2 red peppers
- Juice of 1 lemon
- Extra virgin olive oil
- Salt and pepper q.b.
- Fresh parsley q.b.

Preparation

1. Cooking quinoa: Rinse the quinoa under running cold water, then put it in a pot with twice the volume of water. Bring to a boil, reduce the heat and let simmer for about 15 minutes or until the quinoa is tender. Once cooked, drain the excess water and let cool.
2. Preparation of the peppers: Wash the peppers, remove the seeds and cut into small pieces.
3. Preparation of beans: Rinse and drain the red beans.
4. Preparation of the dressing: In a bowl, mix the lemon juice with olive oil, salt and pepper to taste.
5. Salad assembly: In a large bowl, mix together the cooled quinoa, peppers, red beans and seasoning. Add the chopped parsley and stir again.
6. Preparation for transport: Transfer the salad to an airtight container. This salad is well kept in the refrigerator and can be prepared in advance.

03. WHOLE WHEAT PENNE WITH CHERRY TOMATOES, ROCKET AND TUNA

Preparation time: 10 min
Cooking time: 10 min

Calories: 400 kcal   Protein: 50 g
Fats: 20 g   Carbohydrates: 5 g
Fibres: 10 g   Sugars: 3 g

Ingredients

- 200 grams of who-le-grain pens
- 200 grams of cherry tomatoes
- 1 tin of natural tuna
- 2 handfuls of arugu-la
- Extra virgin olive oil
- Salt and pepper q.b.

Preparation

1. Cooking the pasta: Cook the penne according to the instructions on the package. Once cooked, drain and Passale under cold water to stop cooking. Let them cool.
2. Preparing the tomatoes: Wash the tomatoes and cut them in half.
3. Preparation of tuna: Drain the tuna and crumble with a fork.
4. Dish assembly: In a large bowl, mix the penne, cherry tomatoes, tuna and arugula. Season with olive oil, salt and pepper to taste.
5. Preparation for transport: Transfer everything in an airtight container. This dish is well preserved in the refrigerator and can be prepared in advance.

04. COLD RICE WITH CHICKEN AND VEGETABLES

Preparation time: 20 min
Cooking time: 15 min

Calories: 450 kcal
Fats: 20 g
Fibres: 10 g
Protein: 60 g
Carbohydrates: 5 g
Sugars: 5 g

Ingredients

- 200 grams of basmati rice
- 200 grams of chicken breast
- 1 zucchini
- 1 carrot
- 1 red pepper
- Extra virgin olive oil
- Salt and pepper q.b.

Preparation

1. Cooking rice: Cook the rice according to the instructions on the package. Once cooked, drain and cool it under running cold water. Set aside to cool completely.
2. Cooking the chicken: Cut the chicken breast into cubes. Heat a little oil in a pan and add the chicken. Cook over medium-high heat until it is no longer pink in the center. Let cool.
3. Preparation of vegetables: Wash and cut the zucchini, carrot and pepper into cubes.
4. 4 Dish assembly: In a large bowl, combine cold rice, chicken and vegetables. Add olive oil, salt and pepper to taste and mix well.
5. Preparation for transport: Transfer the rice to an airtight container. This dish is well preserved in the refrigerator and can be prepared in advance.

05. WRAP OF HUMMUS AND VEGETABLES

Preparation time: 10 min
Cooking time: 0 min

Calories: 300 kcal   Protein: 45 g
Fats: 8 g   Carbohydrates: 8 g
Fibres: 10 g   Sugars: 3 g

Ingredients

- 4 tortillas of wheat
- 200 grams of hummus
- 1 red pepper
- 1 carrot
- 2 cucumbers
- 100 grams of fresh spinach leaves

Preparation

1. Preparation of vegetables: Wash and cut the pepper, carrot and cucumbers into strips.
2. Wrap assembly: Spread some hummus on each tortilla. Spread the vegetables and spinach evenly over each tortilla. Wrap the tortillas around the filling, taking care not to fill them too much.
3. Preparation for transport: Wrap each wrap in aluminum foil or kitchen paper to keep it closed. These wraps can be eaten immediately or refrigerated for lunch the next day.

06. PANZANELLA

Preparation time: 15 min
Cooking time: 0 min

Calories: 250 kcal   Protein: 35 g
Fats: 5 g   Carbohydrates: 5 g
Fibres: 10 g   Sugars: 5 g

Ingredients

- 200 grams of stale bread
- 200 grams of ripe tomatoes
- 1 red onion
- Fresh basil q.b.
- Extra virgin olive oil
- Red wine vinegar
- Salt and pepper q.b.

Preparation

1. Bread preparation: Cut the stale bread into cubes and place in a large bowl.
2. Tomatoes preparation: Wash and cut the tomatoes into cubes. Add the tomatoes and their juice to the bread.
3. Preparation of the onion: Finely slice the red onion and add it to the bowl.
4. Dish assembly: Add fresh basil torn by hand. Season with olive oil, red wine vinegar, salt and pepper to taste. Stir well and let it sit for at least an hour so that the flavors mix.
5. Preparation for transport: Transfer the panzanella in an airtight container. This dish is well preserved in the refrigerator and can be prepared in advance.

07. SMOKED SALMON AND WILD RICE SALAD

Preparation time: 15 min
Cooking time: 20 min

Calories: 400 kcal   Protein: 40 g
Fats: 20 g   Carbohydrates: 3 g
Fibres: 15 g   Sugars: 3 g

Ingredients

- 200 grams of wild rice
- 200 grams of smoked salmon
- 1 cucumber
- 2 shallots
- Extra virgin olive oil
- Juice of 1 lemon
- Salt and pepper q.b.
- Fresh dill q.b.

Preparation

1. Cooking rice: Cook the wild rice according to the instructions on the package. Once cooked, drain it and let it cool.
2. 2 Preparing the salmon: Cut the smoked salmon into thin strips.
3. Preparation of the vegetables: Wash the cucumber, cut it in half lengthwise, then into thin slices. Slice the shallots finely.
4. Salad assembly: In a large bowl, combine the cooled rice, salmon, cucumber and shallots. Season with olive oil, lemon juice, salt and pepper to taste. Mix well and garnish with fresh dill.
5. Preparation for transport: Transfer the salad to an airtight container. This salad is well kept in the refrigerator and can be prepared in advance.

NOTE 7 (pg 129)

08. COLD CUCUMBER SOUP AND YOGURT

Preparation time: 10 min
Cooking time: 0 min

Calories: 200 kcal   Protein: 15 g
Fats: 10 g   Carbohydrates: 2 g
Fibres: 10 g   Sugars: 10 g

Ingredients

- 3 large cucumbers
- 500 grams of Greek yogurt
- 2 cloves of garlic
- Juice of 1 lemon
- Extra virgin olive oil
- Salt and pepper q.b.
- Fresh dill q.b.

Preparation

1. Preparing the cucumbers: Wash the cucumbers, cut them in half lengthwise and remove the seeds with a teaspoon. Cut into cubes.
2. Preparation of the soup: In a mixer or blender, combine cucumbers, yogurt, garlic, lemon juice, olive oil, salt and pepper. Blend until smooth. Taste and season with salt and pepper if necessary.
3. Optional addition of cucumbers: If you want to accentuate the flavor of cucumber cut one into rings and add it over the cold soup.
4. Cooling the soup: Put the soup in the refrigerator for at least an hour or until ready to serve.
5. Preparation for transport: Transfer the soup to an airtight container. This soup is well kept in the refrigerator and can be prepared in advance.

TABBOULEH OF QUINOA

Preparation time:	15 min	Calories:	300 kcal
Cooking time:	15 min	Fats:	8 g
		Fibres:	10 g

Protein:	40 g
Carbohydrates:	6 g
Sugars:	3 g

Ingredients

- 200 grams of quinoa
- 200 grams of ripe tomatoes
- 1 cucumber
- 4 spring onions
- Juice of 2 lemons
- Extra virgin olive oil
- Salt and pepper q.b.
- Fresh mint and parsley q.b.

Preparation

1. Cooking quinoa: Cook the quinoa according to the instructions on the package. Once cooked, drain it and let it cool.
2. Preparation of vegetables: Wash and dice the tomatoes and cucumber. Slice the spring onions finely.
3. Assembly of the dish: In a large bowl, combine the cooled quinoa, tomatoes, cucumber and spring onions. Season with olive oil, lemon juice, salt and pepper to taste. Add mint and fresh chopped parsley and mix well.
4. Preparation for transport: Transfer the tabbouleh to an airtight container. This dish is well preserved in the refrigerator and can be prepared in advance.

10. PASTA SALAD WITH FETA AND OLIVES

Preparation time:	20 min	Calories:	400 kcal	Protein:	50 g
Cooking time:	10 min	Fats:	10 g	Carbohydrates:	3 g
		Fibres:	15 g	Sugars:	5 g

Ingredients

- 200 grams of short pasta
- 100 grams of feta
- 100 grams of pitted black olives
- 200 grams of cherry tomatoes
- Extra virgin olive oil
- Salt and pepper q.b.

Preparation

1. Cooking the pasta: Cook the pasta according to the instructions on the package. Once cooked, drain and cool under cold running water.
2. Preparation of the ingredients: Cut the feta into cubes, cut the black olives into slices and cut the tomatoes in half.
3. Assembly of the dish: In a large bowl, combine the cooled pasta, feta, olives and cherry tomatoes. Season with olive oil, salt and pepper to taste. Mix well.
4. Preparation for transport: Transfer the salad to an airtight container. This dish is well preserved in the refrigerator and can be prepared in advance.

11. VEGETABLE OMELETTE

| Preparation time: | 10 min |
| Cooking time: | 20 min |

Calories:	200 kcal	Protein:	5 g
Fats:	12 g	Carbohydrates:	2 g
Fibres:	15 g	Sugars:	2 g

Ingredients

- 6 eggs
- 1 zucchini
- 1 red pepper
- 1 onion
- Extra virgin olive oil
- Salt and pepper q.b.

Preparation

1. Preparation of the vegetables: Wash and dice the zucchini and pepper. Slice the onion finely.
2. Cooking the vegetables: Heat a little oil in a pan and fry the onion until it becomes transparent. Add the zucchini and pepper and cook until tender.
3. Preparing the omelet: In a bowl, beat the eggs with salt and pepper. Pour the beaten eggs over the vegetables in the pan. Cook over medium heat until the eggs are fully cooked.
4. Preparation for transport: Let the omelette cool, then cut it into slices and transfer to an airtight container. This dish is well preserved in the refrigerator and can be prepared in advance.

12. SALAD OF GREEK CHICKEN

Preparation time: 20 min
Cooking time: 15 min

Calories: 400 kcal   Protein: 20 g
Fats: 30 g   Carbohydrates: 5 g
Fibres: 20 g   Sugars: 5 g

Ingredients

- 2 grilled chicken breasts
- 200 grams of romaine lettuce
- 100 grams of cherry tomatoes
- 1 cucumber
- 100 grams of feta
- 100 grams of pitted black olives
- Extra virgin olive oil
- Juice of 1 lemon
- Salt and pepper q.b.

Preparation

1. Preparation of ingredients: Cut the grilled chicken into thin strips. Wash and cut the lettuce into strips. Cut the tomatoes in half, the cucumber into slices and the feta into cubes.
2. Salad mixture: Combine chicken, lettuce, cherry tomatoes, cucumber, feta cheese and olives in a large bowl. Season with olive oil, lemon juice, salt and pepper to taste. Mix well.
3. Preparation for transport: Transfer the salad to an airtight container. This salad is well kept in the refrigerator and can be prepared in advance.

13. COLD RICE WITH GRILLED VEGETABLES AND TUNA

Preparation time: 20 min
Cooking time: 15 min

Calories: 400 kcal
Fats: 20 g
Fibres: 10 g
Protein: 50 g
Carbohydrates: 5 g
Sugars: 5 g

Ingredients

- 200 grams of rice
- 1 zucchini
- 1 red pepper
- 1 carrot
- 1 can of tuna
- Extra virgin olive oil
- Salt and pepper q.b.

Preparation

1. Cooking rice: Cook the rice according to the instructions on the package. Once cooked, drain it and let it cool.
2. Grilling vegetables: Wash and slice the vegetables. Lightly grease with olive oil and grill on a grill or a grill pan until they are tender and have nice grilled streaks.
3. Dish assembly: In a large bowl, combine the cooled rice, grilled vegetables and the crumbled tuna. Season with olive oil, salt and pepper to taste. Mix well.
4. Preparation for transport: Transfer the cold rice to an airtight container. This dish is well preserved in the refrigerator and can be prepared in advance.

14. PASTA FREDDA WITH ROCKET PESTO

Preparation time: 15 min
Cooking time: 10 min

Calories: 400 kcal   Protein: 40 g
Fats: 12 g   Carbohydrates: 5 g
Fibres: 25 g   Sugars: 2 g

Ingredients

- 200 grams of short pasta
- 200 grams of arugula
- 50 grams of almonds
- 1 clove of garlic
- 50 grams of Parmesan cheese
- Extra virgin olive oil
- Salt and pepper q.b.

Preparation

1. Cooking the pasta: Cook the pasta according to the instructions on the package. Once cooked, drain and cool under cold running water.
2. Preparation of pesto: In the blender, combine the arugula, almonds, garlic and parmesan cheese. While whisking, add olive oil until creamy. Taste and season with salt and pepper if necessary.
3. Dish assembly: In a large bowl, combine the cooled pasta and pesto. Stir well until the dough is completely covered with pesto.

15. ROLLED OMELETTE WITH SPINACH AND RICOTTA

Preparation time: 10 min
Cooking time: 10 min

Calories:	350 kcal	Protein:	6 g
Fats:	20 g	Carbohydrates:	3 g
Fibres:	25 g	Sugars:	2 g

Ingredients

- 4 eggs
- 200 grams of fresh spinach
- 100 grams of ricotta cheese
- Extra virgin olive oil
- Salt and pepper q.b.

Preparation

1. Preparing the spinach: In a non-stick pan, cook the spinach with a little olive oil until they wilt. Drain any excess liquid.
2. Preparing the omelet: In a bowl, beat the eggs with a little salt and pepper. Pour the eggs into a non-stick pan and cook over medium heat until the eggs are no longer liquid.
3. Omelette assembly: Spread the cooked spinach and ricotta on the omelet. Roll up the omelet carefully and let it cool.
4. Preparation for transport: Cut the omelet into slices and transfer to an airtight container. This dish is well preserved in the refrigerator and can be prepared in advance.

16. BARLEY SALAD WITH TOMATOES AND OLIVES

Preparation time: 15 min
Cooking time: 20 min

Calories: 300 kcal Protein: 45 g
Fats: 8 g Carbohydrates: 5 g
Fibres: 10 g Sugars: 3 g

Ingredients

- 200 grams of barley
- 200 grams of cherry tomatoes
- 100 grams of pitted black olives
- Juice of 1 lemon
- Extra virgin olive oil
- Salt and pepper q.b.

Preparation

1. Cooking barley: Cook barley according to the instructions on the package. Once cooked, drain and let it cool.
2. Preparation of the ingredients: Cut the tomatoes in half and cut the olives into slices.
3. Salad assembly: In a large bowl, combine the cooled barley, tomatoes and olives. Season with olive oil, lemon juice, salt and pepper to taste. Mix well.
4. Preparation for transport: Transfer the salad to an airtight container. This salad is well kept in the refrigerator and can be prepared in advance.

17. CHICKEN TERIYAKI WITH RICE

Preparation time: 15 min
Cooking time: 20 min

Calories: 550 kcal
Fats: 35 g
Fibres: 15 g

Protein: 70 g
Carbohydrates: 5 g
Sugars: 5 g

Ingredients

- 2 chicken breasts
- 200 grams of basmati rice
- 4 tablespoons of teriyaki sauce
- 2 tablespoons of sesame oil
- 1 broccoli
- Sesame seeds for garnish

Preparation

1. Cooking rice: Cook basmati rice according to the instructions on the package. Once cooked, let it cool.
2. Preparation of the teriyaki chicken: In a pan, cook the chicken breasts with sesame oil until golden brown. Add the teriyaki sauce and cook for another 5 minutes.
3. Preparation of the broccoli: Meanwhile, wash and cut the broccoli into florets and steam until it becomes tender.
4. Dish assembly: Place the rice, teriyaki chicken and broccoli in a container. Sprinkle with sesame seeds.

18. SALAD BOWL OF QUINOA AND AVOCADO

Preparation time: 15 min
Cooking time: 15 min

Calories: 400 kcal Protein: 50 g
Fats: 10 g Carbohydrates: 10 g
Fibres: 20 g Sugars: 5 g

Ingredients

- 200 grams of quinoa
- 1 ripe avocado
- 200 grams of cherry tomatoes
- 1 cucumber
- Juice of 1 lemon
- Extra virgin olive oil
- Salt and pepper q.b.

Preparation

1. Cooking quinoa: Cook the quinoa according to the instructions on the package. Once cooked, let it cool.
2. Preparation of the vegetables: Cut the avocado, cherry tomatoes and cucumber into cubes.
3. Salad bowl assembly: Place quinoa, avocado, cherry tomatoes and cucumber in a container. Season with lemon juice, olive oil, salt and pepper.

19. TUNA AND CUCUMBER SANDWICH

Preparation time: 10 min
Cooking time: 0 min

Calories: 350 kcal   Protein: 40 g
Fats: 20 g   Carbohydrates: 5 g
Fibres: 10 g   Sugars: 5 g

Ingredients

- 2 slices of whole-meal bread
- 1 can of tuna
- 1 cucumber
- 2 tablespoons of light mayonnaise
- Salt and pepper q.b.

Preparation

1. Preparing the filling: Drain the tuna and put it in a bowl. Add the mayonnaise and mix well.
2. Preparing the sandwich: Toast the slices of bread. Spread the tuna on a slice of bread, add the sliced cucumber and season with salt and pepper. Cover with the other slice of bread.
3. Preparation for transport: Wrap the sandwich in aluminum foil or plastic wrap to keep it tightly closed. This sandwich is well preserved and can be prepared in advance.

20. BULGUR'S TABBOULEH WITH TOMATOES AND MINT

Preparation time: 15 min
Cooking time: 15 min

Calories: 350 kcal   Protein: 45 g
Fats: 7 g   Carbohydrates: 7 g
Fibres: 15 g   Sugars: 5 g

Ingredients

- 200 grams of bulgur
- 200 grams of ripe but firm tomatoes
- 1 bunch of fresh parsley
- 1 bunch of fresh mint
- 4 tablespoons of extra virgin olive oil
- Juice of 2 lemons
- Salt q.b.

Preparation

1. Cooking the bulgur: Put the bulgur in a bowl and cover it with boiling water. Leave to soak for 20 minutes or until the bulgur becomes soft. Drain the excess water and let cool.
2. Preparation of the vegetables: Wash the tomatoes carefully, then cut them in half or in quarters, depending on the size. Wash and finely chop the parsley and mint, taking care to remove the larger stems.
3. Dish assembly: In a large bowl, combine the cooled bulgur, chopped cherry tomatoes, chopped parsley and mint. Add olive oil, lemon juice and salt to taste, then mix well to make sure all the ingredients are well blended.
4. Preparation for transport: Transfer the tabbouleh to an airtight container. This dish is well preserved in the refrigerator and can be prepared in advance.

21. BLACK RICE SALAD WITH SHRIMP AND MANGO

Preparation time: 20 min
Cooking time: 20 min

Calories: 500 kcal
Fats: 15 g
Fibres: 15 g
Protein: 75 g
Carbohydrates: 5 g
Sugars: 15 g

Ingredients

- 200 grams of black rice
- 200 grams of peeled shrimps
- 1 ripe mango
- Juice of 1 lime
- 3 tablespoons of extra virgin olive oil
- Salt and pepper q.b.

Preparation

1. Cooking rice and shrimps: Cook the black rice in salted boiling water for the time indicated on the package, then drain and cool under cold water. Meanwhile, cook the shrimps in boiling water for 2-3 minutes, then drain them and let them cool.
2. Preparation of mango: Peel the mango, cut it in half, remove the core and cut the pulp into cubes.
3. Salad assembly: In a bowl, combine the cooled black rice, cooled shrimps and mango cubes. Season with lime juice, olive oil and salt and pepper to taste.
4. Preparation for transport: Transfer the rice salad to an airtight container. This dish is well preserved in the refrigerator and can be prepared in advance.

22. WRAP OF CHICKEN CAESAR STYLE

Preparation time: 15min
Cooking time: 0min

Calories: 400kcal Protein: 40g
Fats: 25g Carbohydrates: 5g
Fibres: 15g Sugars: 2g

Ingredients

- 2 wraps of whole wheat
- 2 chicken breasts
- Romaine lettuce
- 50 grams of grated parmesan cheese
- Caesar sauce light
- Extra virgin olive oil
- Salt and pepper q.b.

Preparation

1. Cooking the chicken: Heat a little oil in a pan and cook the chicken breasts over medium-high heat, seasoning with salt and pepper. Once cooked, let them cool before cutting them into thin slices.
2. Preparation of lettuce: Wash the Roman lettuce leaves and tear them into smaller pieces.
3. Wrap assembly: Spread a generous amount of Caesar sauce on each wrap. Spread the lettuce and chicken evenly over each wrap. Sprinkle with grated Parmesan.
4. Roll and prepare for transport: Roll each wrap carefully, making sure the filling stays inside. Wrap each wrap in aluminum foil or plastic wrap. These wraps are well preserved and can be prepared in advance.

23. BAKED SALMON WITH QUINOA SALAD

| Preparation time: | 20 min |
| Cooking time: | 20 min |

Calories:	550 kcal	Protein:	45 g
Fats:	30 g	Carbohydrates:	7 g
Fibres:	25 g	Sugars:	2 g

Ingredients

- 2 slices of salmon
- 200 grams of quinoa
- 1 bunch of aspara-gus
- Juice of 1 lemon
- 3 tablespoons of extra virgin olive oil
- Salt and pepper q.b.

Preparation

1. Cooking salmon: Preheat the oven to 200 °C. Place the salmon slices on a baking sheet lined with baking paper, sprinkle with a tablespoon of olive oil and season with salt and pepper. Bake for about 15 minutes, or until the salmon is cooked to perfection.
2. Cooking quinoa and asparagus: Meanwhile, cook the quinoa as indicated on the package. Cut the woody part of the asparagus and steam them until tender.
3. Assembly of the dish: In a large bowl, combine the cooked quinoa, asparagus and salmon crumbled. Season with olive oil and lemon juice, then stir gently to combine.
4. Preparation for transport: Transfer the quinoa and salmon salad to an airtight container. This dish is well preserved in the refrigerator and can be prepared in advance.

PASTA FREDDA WITH CHERRY TOMATOES, OLIVES AND SALTED RICOTTA

Preparation time:	15 min		
Cooking time:	10 min		

Calories:	550 kcal	Protein:	50 g
Fats:	15 g	Carbohydrates:	5 g
Fibres:	30 g	Sugars:	2 g

Ingredients

- 200 g short pasta (e.g. butterflies, penne)
- 200 grams of cherry tomatoes
- 100 grams of pitted black olives
- 100 grams of salted ricotta
- 3 tablespoons of extra virgin olive oil
- Salt q.b.

Preparation

1. Cooking the pasta: Cook the pasta in salted boiling water according to the instructions on the package. Drain the pasta and pass it under cold water to stop cooking and cool quickly.
2. Preparation of the ingredients: Cut the tomatoes in half, cut the olives into rounds and grate the ricotta.
3. Dish assembly: In a large bowl, combine the cooled pasta, cherry tomatoes, olives and salted ricotta. Season with olive oil and salt, stirring well to mix all the ingredients.
4. Preparation for transport: Transfer the cold dough to an airtight container. This dish is well preserved in the refrigerator and can be prepared in advance.

25. COLD PASTA SALAD WITH VEGETABLES AND FETA

Preparation time: 20 min
Cooking time: 15 min

Calories: 400 kcal
Fats: 15 g
Fibres: 15 g

Protein: 50 g
Carbohydrates: 7 g
Sugars: 5 g

Ingredients

- 200g of short who-lemeal pasta
- 1 red pepper
- 1 zucchini
- 200g of cherry to-matoes
- 100g of feta cheese
- Olive oil, salt, pep-per and oregano to taste

Preparation

1. Cooking Pasta: Boil a pot of salted water and cook the pasta according to the in-structions on the package. Once cooked, drain and pass under cold water to stop cooking and cool.
2. Preparation of Vegetables: Cut the pepper and zucchini into cubes and cut the to-matoes in half.
3. Salad Assembly: In a large bowl, combine pasta, vegetables, and feta cut into cu-bes. Season with olive oil, salt, pepper and oregano to taste. Mix well to mix all ingredients.

NOTE 25 (pg 131)

AUTUMN

01. BUTTERNUT PUMPKIN AND CARROT SOUP WITH GARLIC CROUTONS

Preparation time:	20 min	Calories:	200 kcal	Protein:	4 g
Cooking time:	30 min	Fats:	8 g	Carbohydrates:	30 g
		Fibres:	6 g	Sugars:	8 g

Ingredients

- 500g of pumpkin Butternut
- 300g of carrots
- 2 cloves of garlic
- 4 slices of whole-meal bread
- Extra virgin olive oil q.b.
- Salt and pepper q.b.
- 1 liter of vegetable broth
- Grated parmesan cheese (optional)

Preparation

1. Preparation of ingredients: Peel the Butternut pumpkin and cut into cubes. Peel the carrots and cut them into thin slices. Finely chop one clove of garlic and cut the other clove in half.
2. Cooking the vegetables: In a large pot, add a drizzle of olive oil and sauté the chopped garlic clove over low heat until golden brown. Add the pumpkin and carrots, then stir to add the oil and garlic. Add the vegetable stock to cover the vegetables and bring to a boil. Reduce the heat to medium-low and cook for about 20-25 minutes, or until the pumpkin and carrots become soft but do not flake.
3. Preparation of the croutons: While the vegetables are cooking, preheat the oven to 180 º C. Spread a little olive oil on both sides of the slices of wholemeal bread and rub the half of the clove of garlic cut on one side of the slices. Place the croutons on a baking tray and bake for about 5-7 minutes, or until they become crispy and slightly golden.
4. Blend the soup: Once the pumpkin and carrots are cooked, remove the whole garlic from the pot. Using an immersion blender, blend the vegetables until you get a velvety consistency. Adjust the salt and pepper to your taste.

NOTE 1 (pg 132)

AUTUMN

73

BAKED SWEET POTATOES WITH ROSEMARY AND NUTS

Preparation time: 10 min
Cooking time: 30 min

Calories: 250 kcal   Protein: 4 g
Fats: 10 g   Carbohydrates: 35 g
Fibres: 6 g   Sugars: 8 g

Ingredients

- 500g of sweet potatoes
- 2 tablespoons of extra virgin olive oil
- 2 sprigs of fresh rosemary
- 1/2 teaspoon of salt
- Red chili powder (optional)
- 30g of chopped nuts
- Grated rind of 1 lemon

Preparation

1. Preparing the potatoes: Preheat the oven to 200 ºC. Peel the sweet potatoes and dice them about 2 cm. Make sure the cubes are all the same size for even cooking.
2. Marinade with flavors: In a large bowl, mix the sweet potato cubes with the extra virgin olive oil, chopped rosemary leaves, salt and, if desired, a pinch of red chili powder for a touch of spiciness. Let the potatoes marinate for about 5 minutes, so that the aromas are well impregnated.
3. Baking in the oven: Place the potato cubes on a baking sheet lined with baking paper, making sure to distribute them evenly. Bake the potatoes for about 30-35 minutes or until tender and lightly browned outside.
4. Roasting the nuts: Meanwhile, in a non-stick pan, toast the chopped nuts over medium heat for about 3-4 minutes, stirring occasionally, until they release an aromatic scent. Keep an eye on the nuts to prevent them from burning.
5. Final dressing: Once the sweet potatoes are cooked, transfer them to a serving bowl and sprinkle with toasted walnuts and grated lemon peel. Stir gently to evenly distribute the seasonings.

03. STUFFED CHEESE AND PARSLEY MUSHROOMS

Preparation time:	20 min		Calories:	200 kcal	Protein:	4 g
Cooking time:	30 min		Fats:	8 g	Carbohydrates:	30 g
			Fibres:	6 g	Sugars:	8 g

Ingredients

- 6 large mushrooms (porcini or champignon)
- 100g cream cheese (e.g. philadelphia)
- 1 bunch of fresh parsley
- 2 tablespoons of breadcrumbs
- 2 tablespoons grated Parmesan cheese
- 1 clove of garlic (optional)
- Extra virgin olive oil
- Salt and pepper q.b.

Preparation

1. Cleaning the mushrooms: Start by gently cleaning the mushrooms with a damp cloth to remove any soil residue. Remove the stems from the hats, emptying them slightly in the center to create the space of the filling.
2. Preparation of the filling: In a bowl, mix the cream cheese with finely chopped parsley, breadcrumbs, grated Parmesan cheese and, if desired, a finely chopped clove of garlic. Season with salt and pepper to taste and stir until smooth.
3. Filling the mushrooms: Fill the mushroom hats with the cheese and parsley mixture, pressing lightly to make the filling stick.
4. Baking: Place the stuffed mushrooms on a baking sheet lined with baking paper. Sprinkle a little extra virgin olive oil on the mushrooms to make them softer and golden. Bake at 180 ºC for about 15-20 minutes or until the mushrooms are well cooked and the filling is golden on the surface.

NOTE 3 (pg 132)

04. CARAMELIZED PEARS WITH GORGONZOLA CHEESE AND HONEY

Preparation time: 10 min
Cooking time: 15 min

Calories:	200 kcal	Protein:	6 g
Fats:	10 g	Carbohydrates:	25 g
Fibres:	4 g	Sugars:	18 g

Ingredients

- 2 pears ripe but still firm
- 50g of Gorgonzola cheese
- 2 tablespoons of honey
- 20g of butter
- Black pepper powder q.b.

Preparation

1. Preparing pears: Start by washing and drying pears. Cut them in half lengthwise and, with a teaspoon, gently remove the seeds and part of the central core to create a cavity for the filling.
2. Filling the pears: Cut the Gorgonzola cheese into small pieces and distribute it inside the cavities of the pears, trying to make the cheese stick well to the pulp.
3. Cooking the pears: In a non-stick pan, melt the butter over medium heat. Arrange the stuffed pears in the pan with the cut side down. Let the pears cook for about 7-8 minutes or until the lower part becomes golden and caramelized.
4. Pear caramelization: Add the honey to the caramelized pears, spreading it evenly over the surface of the pears. Continue cooking for another 3-4 minutes or until the honey caramelizes slightly and the pears become soft and juicy.

NOTE 4 (pg 132)

05. GRAPES AND CRUNCHY NUTS WITH CHEDDAR CHEESE

Preparation time: 10 min
Cooking time: 0 min

Calories: kcal   Protein: g
Fats: g   Carbohydrates: g
Fibres: g   Sugars: g

Ingredients

- 200g white or black grapes, washed and dried
- 50g of shelled walnuts
- 100g cheddar cheese, cut into cubes
- 2 tablespoons of honey
- Pinch of salt

Preparation

1. Preparation of the grapes: Divide the grapes into grains and remove the seeds, if any. Let the beans dry on paper towels.
2. Roasting the nuts: In a non-stick pan, toast the shelled nuts over medium heat for about 3-4 minutes, or until they become fragrant and slightly golden. Cool them on a plate.
3. Salad assembly: In a bowl, combine the grapes, roasted nuts and cheddar cheese cubes. Stir gently to distribute the ingredients evenly.
4. Seasoning: Add honey to the mixture of grapes, nuts and cheese. Add a pinch of salt to balance the flavors.

NOTE 5 (pg 132)

06. FIGS WITH PROSCIUTTO, ARUGULA AND BALSAMIC VINEGAR

Preparation time: 10 min
Cooking time: 0 min

Calories: 180 kcal   Protein: 8 g
Fats: 10 g   Carbohydrates: 15 g
Fibres: 2 g   Sugars: 12 g

Ingredients

- 8 fresh figs, ripe but not too soft
- 8 thin slices of raw ham
- 80g of fresh rocket
- 2 tablespoons of balsamic vinegar
- Pinch of ground black pepper

Preparation

1. Preparation of figs: Wash the figs gently under running water and dry them with a clean cloth. Cut the top of each fig, about 1 cm from the top, then cut the top of the figs forming a shallow cross.
2. Wrapping with raw ham: Take a slice of raw ham and wrap it around each fig, so as to cover the top and keep the incision at the top. Make sure the ham covers the figs stably, but not too tight.
3. Salad assembly: Arrange the arugula in a serving plate or in individual portions. Place the figs wrapped in the ham on top of the arugula to create an attractive presentation.
4. Dressing with balsamic vinegar: Spray the balsamic vinegar over the figs and arugula. Add a pinch of ground black pepper to give it a touch of flavor.

HAZELNUT, CAULIFLOWER AND RAISIN SALAD WITH LEMON DRESSING

Preparation time: 15 min
Cooking time: 10 min

Calories:	300 kcal	Protein:	8 g
Fats:	20 g	Carbohydrates:	25 g
Fibres:	6 g	Sugars:	12 g

Ingredients

- 200g of cauliflower
- 50g of roasted and shelled hazelnuts
- 30g of sultanas raisins
- 1 lemon (juice and grated rind)
- 2 tablespoons of extra virgin olive oil
- Salt and pepper q.b.

Preparation

1. Cauliflower preparation: Divide the cauliflower into small florets and rinse under running water. Drain and dry thoroughly with a cloth or paper towel.
2. Cooking cauliflower: Heat a large pan over medium heat and add a tablespoon of olive oil. Add cauliflower and Cuocilo for 5-7 minutes or until tender, but keep a nice crunch. Add salt and pepper to taste.
3. Preparation of the dressing: In a bowl, mix the lemon juice, the grated lemon peel and a tablespoon of olive oil. Add salt and pepper to taste.
4. Salad assembly: In a large bowl, combine the cooked cauliflower, roasted and shelled hazelnuts, and sultanas. Pour the lemon dressing over the mixture and stir gently to distribute the dressing evenly.

NOTE 7 (pg 132)

08. CARROTS GLAZED WITH HONEY AND GINGER

Preparation time: 10 min
Cooking time: 20 min

Calories: 150 kcal   Protein: 2 g
Fats: 5 g   Carbohydrates: 25 g
Fibres: 4 g   Sugars: 20 g

Ingredients

- 500g of carrots
- 2 tablespoons of honey
- 1 tablespoon grated fresh ginger
- 1 tablespoon of olive oil
- Salt and pepper q.b.

Preparation

1. Preparation of the carrots: Peel the carrots and cut them into sticks or slices, to taste. Make sure the carrots are similar in size for even cooking.
2. Cooking the carrots: In a large pan, heat the olive oil over medium heat. Add the carrots and cook for 5-7 minutes, until they begin to brown slightly.
3. Preparation of the icing: In a bowl, mix the honey and grated ginger until you get a homogeneous glaze.
4. Adding icing: Pour the honey and ginger icing over the carrots into the pan and stir well to distribute evenly. Continue to cook for another 5-7 minutes or until the carrots become tender and caramelized.
5. Service: Transfer the glazed carrots to a serving dish and add salt and pepper to taste.

09. KALE TART AND CARAMELIZED ONIONS

Preparation time: 30 min
Cooking time: 30 min

Calories: 300 kcal   Protein: 5 g
Fats: 15 g   Carbohydrates: 35 g
Fibres: 5 g   Sugars: 6 g

Ingredients

- 200g of flour 00
- 100g of cold butter cubes
- 1 egg yolk
- 2-3 tablespoons of cold water
- 300g of kale
- 2 large onions
- 2 tablespoons of olive oil
- 1 tablespoon of balsamic vinegar
- Salt q.b.

Preparation

1. Preparation of the base of the tart: In a bowl, combine the flour and cold butter cubes. With your hands, work the ingredients into a sandy mixture. Add the egg yolk and cold water, one tablespoon at a time, and continue to work until a smooth dough forms. Wrap the dough in cling film and let it rest in the fridge for at least 30 minutes.
2. Preparation of the filling: Slice the kale and onions thinly. In a large frying pan, heat the olive oil over medium heat and add the onions. Caramellalele until soft and slightly golden. Add the sliced kale and continue cooking until the cabbage softens. Add the balsamic vinegar, salt and pepper to taste and mix well. Turn off the heat and leave aside.
3. Preparation of the tart: Preheat the oven to 180 °C (350 °F). Take the dough from the film and spread it on a floured surface with the help of a rolling pin. Transfer the spread dough to a tart pan about 20-22 cm in diameter and fit the shape. Prick the bottom of the tart with a fork and add the filling of cabbage and onions.
4. Baking the tart: Bake the tart and cook for about 25-30 minutes or until the base becomes golden and crispy.
5. Service: Allow the tart to cool slightly before taking it to work.

NOTE 9 (pg 132)

AUTUMN

10. CHARD AND FETA OMELETTE WITH CHERRY TOMATOES

Preparation time: 15 min
Cooking time: 15 min

Calories: 150 kcal Protein: 18 g
Fats: 15 g Carbohydrates: 6 g
Fibres: 2 g Sugars: 3 g

Ingredients

- 6 eggs
- 200g of fresh beets
- 100g of feta cheese
- 10 cherry tomatoes
- 1 clove of garlic
- Olive oil
- Salt and pepper q.b.

Preparation

1. Preparation of the chard: Wash the chard thoroughly under running water. Separate the leaves from the stems and cut the leaves into thin strips. Cut the stems into small pieces.
2. Cooking the chard: In a pan, heat a little olive oil and the crushed garlic over medium heat. Add the chard stems and cook for a few minutes until soft. Add the chard leaves and cook until they wilt and reduce in volume. Season with salt and pepper. Turn off the heat and let the beets cool.
3. Preparation of cherry tomatoes: Cut the cherry tomatoes in half.
4. Preparation of the omelette: In a bowl, beat the eggs with a pinch of salt and pepper. Add the cooled chard and the cherry tomatoes cut in half. Crumble the feta on the egg and vegetable mixture.
5. Cooking the omelette: Heat a non-stick pan with a little olive oil over medium heat. Pour the mixture of eggs, vegetables and feta into the pan and level the surface. Cover with a lid and cook for about 5-7 minutes or until the omelet solidifies on the edges. With the help of a plate flip the omelette and cook for another 5-7 minutes until it is completely cooked and golden brown.
6. Service: Cut the omelette into wedges and serve hot or cold

11. KALE TART AND CARAMELIZED ONIONS

Preparation time: 15 min
Cooking time: 30 min

Calories: 250 kcal
Fats: 15 g
Fibres: 3 g
Protein: 5 g
Carbohydrates: 30 g
Sugars: 10 g

Ingredients

- 1 roll of brisée pastry (about 230g)
- 200g of curly cabbage
- 2 large onions
- 2 tablespoons of brown sugar
- 2 tablespoons of apple cider vinegar
- 2 tablespoons of olive oil
- Salt and pepper q.b.

Preparation

1. Preparation of kale: Thoroughly wash the kale, remove the center core and cut the leaves into thin strips.
2. Cooking the kale: In a large pan, heat the olive oil over medium heat. Add the chopped kale and cook until soft and wilt. Adjust the flavor with salt and pepper, then let cool.
3. Caramelizing the onions: Cut the onions into thin slices and cook them slowly in a separate pan with olive oil, until they become transparent and soft. Add brown sugar and apple cider vinegar and cook until caramelized onions are obtained. Let cool.
4. Preparation of the tart: Preheat the oven to 180 °C, then roll out the brisée dough in a tart pan, making sure to cover the bottom and edges well. Prick the bottom slightly with a fork.
5. Assembly of the tart: Distribute the kale cooked evenly on the basis of the tart, then arrange the caramelized onions over the cabbage.
6. Baking the tart: Bake and cook for about 25-30 minutes, or until the dough is golden brown.
7. Service: Cut the omelette into wedges and serve hot or cold

AUTUMN

12. ROASTED BRUSSELS SPROUTS WITH ALMONDS AND GARLIC

Preparation time: 15 min
Cooking time: 20 min

Calories: 350 kcal Protein: 12 g
Fats: 20 g Carbohydrates: 30 g
Fibres: 8 g Sugars: 5 g

Ingredients

- 500g of Brussels sprouts
- 100g of almonds
- 2 cloves of garlic
- Olive oil, salt and pepper q.b.

Preparation

1. Preparing the sprouts: Clean the Brussels sprouts by removing the outer leaves and cutting them in half.
2. Preparation of almonds and garlic: Chop the almonds and garlic finely.
3. Cooking the sprouts: In a pan, heat a little olive oil and add the Brussels sprouts. Cook over medium heat for about 10 minutes, until they begin to brown.
4. Adding almonds and garlic: Add the chopped almonds and garlic to the Brussels sprouts in the pan. Cook for another 10 minutes, stirring occasionally, until the almonds are toasted and the sprouts are tender.
5. Preparation for transport: Transfer the roasted Brussels sprouts with almonds and garlic to an airtight container and refrigerate until lunch.

13. FENNEL GRATIN WITH BÉCHAMEL AND PARMESAN

Preparation time: 15 min
Cooking time: 30 min

Calories: 300 kcal Protein: 12 g
Fats: 15 g Carbohydrates: 25 g
Fibres: 5 g Sugars: 4 g

Ingredients

- 500g of fennel
- 250g of béchamel sauce
- 100g of grated Parmesan cheese
- Salt and pepper q.b.

Preparation

1. Preparation of fennel: Clean the fennel by removing the hard outer part and cutting it into thin slices.
2. Cooking fennel: In a saucepan with salted water, cook the fennel for about 10 minutes, until tender. Drain and let cool.
3. Gratin preparation: Pre-heats the oven to 200 degrees. In a baking dish, arrange the fennel, cover with béchamel and sprinkle with grated Parmesan cheese. Bake for about 20 minutes, or until the cheese is golden and crunchy.
4. Preparation for transport: Once cooled, transfer the fennel gratin to an airtight container and keep in the fridge until lunch.

NOTE 13 (pg 132)

14. STUFFED ONIONS WITH RICE AND PORCINI MUSHROOMS

Preparation time:	20 min	Calories:	350 kcal	Protein:	7 g
Cooking time:	40 min	Fats:	5 g	Carbohydrates:	70 g
		Fibres:	3 g	Sugars:	6 g

Ingredients

- 4 large onions
- 200g of carnaroli rice
- 50g of dried porcini mushrooms
- 2 cloves of garlic
- Olive oil, salt and pepper q.b.

Preparation

1. Preparation of onions: Cut the top of the onions and drain them with the help of a spoon, leaving a shell about 1 cm thick. Preserve the extracted pulp.
2. Preparation of the rice: In a pan, fry the garlic in a little oil. Add the onion pulp and the mushrooms previously soaked and wrung out. After a few minutes, add the rice and let it toast for a few minutes. Cover with water and cook for about 15 minutes. Salt and pepper rule.
3. Filling the onions: Fill the onions with the prepared rice and place them on a baking sheet. Bake at 180 °C for about 20-25 minutes, until the onions become tender.
4. Preparation for transport: Once cooled, transfer the onions to an airtight container and refrigerate until lunch.

15. PEPPERS STUFFED WITH COUSCOUS AND VEGETABLES

Preparation time:	20 min
Cooking time:	30 min

Calories:	300 kcal	Protein:	8 g
Fats:	4 g	Carbohydrates:	50 g
Fibres:	5 g	Sugars:	10 g

Ingredients

- 2 large peppers
- 150g of couscous
- 200g mixed vegetables (carrots, zucchini, eggplant)
- Olive oil, salt and pepper q.b.

Preparation

1. Preparation of the peppers: Cut the top of the peppers and remove the inner seeds. Keep the lids for cooking.
2. Preparing the couscous: Pour the couscous into a bowl and cover with boiling water according to the instructions on the package. Let it rest for about 5 minutes, then peel with a fork.
3. Cooking the vegetables: Cut the vegetables into cubes and cook them in a pan with a little oil until they become tender. Add the couscous to the vegetables and season with salt and pepper.
4. Filling the peppers: Fill the peppers with the couscous and vegetable mix, put the lid on and bake at 180°C for about 20-25 minutes, until the peppers become tender.
5. Preparation for transport: Once cooled, transfer the peppers to an airtight container and refrigerate until lunch.

NOTE 15 (pg 132)

16. CELERY IN WALNUT AND LEMON SAUCE

Preparation time: 20 min
Cooking time: 0 min

Calories: 200 kcal   Protein: 5 g
Fats: 20 g   Carbohydrates: 5 g
Fibres: 3 g   Sugars: 2 g

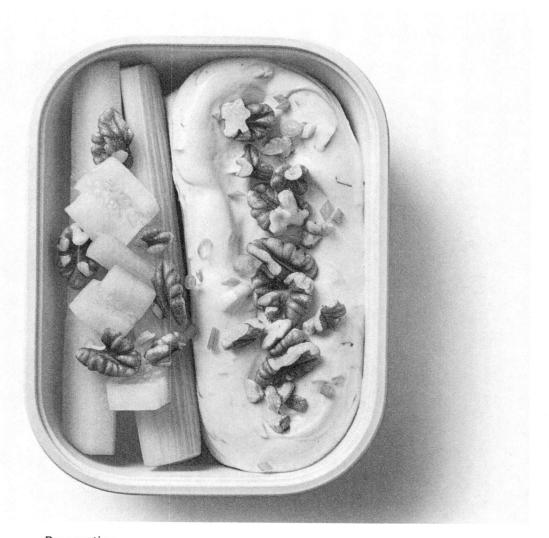

Ingredients

- 1 bunch of celery
- 100g of nuts
- Juice and zest of 1 lemon
- 100ml of extra virgin olive oil
- Salt q.b.

Preparation

1. Cleaning the celery: Wash the celery well, remove any filaments and cut the stems into sticks of about 8-10 cm.
2. Preparation of the sauce: Put the nuts in a mixer, add the lemon juice and zest, olive oil and a pinch of salt. Blend until smooth.
3. Assembly of the dish: Distribute the walnut and lemon sauce on the celery and mix well to make the sauce stick to the stems.
4. Preparation for transport: Transfer the celery into the sauce in an airtight container and keep in the fridge until lunch.

BAKED TURNIPS WITH ROSEMARY AND GARLIC

Preparation time: 15 min
Cooking time: 35 min

Calories: 150 kcal   Protein: 2 g
Fats: 10 g   Carbohydrates: 10 g
Fibres: 3 g   Sugars: 3 g

Ingredients

- 500g of turnips
- 2 branches of rosemary
- 2 cloves of garlic
- Olive oil, salt and pepper q.b.

Preparation

1. Preparation of turnips: Clean the turnips well, cut them into small pieces and dry them with a clean cloth.
2. Dressing the turnips: In a bowl, season the turnips with olive oil, chopped rosemary, crushed garlic, salt and pepper.
3. Cooking the turnips: Arrange the seasoned turnips on a baking sheet covered with baking paper. Bake in a preheated oven at 200 ºC for about 35 minutes, or until they become golden and crunchy.
4. Preparation for transport: Allow the turnips to cool, then transfer them to an airtight container and store in the fridge until lunch.

NOTE 17 (pg 132)

18. SPINACH SAUTEED WITH PINE NUTS AND RAISINS

Preparation time: 10 min
Cooking time: 10 min

Calories: 200 kcal Protein: 5 g
Fats: 10 g Carbohydrates: 25 g
Fibres: 4 g Sugars: 5 g

Ingredients

- 400g of fresh spinach
- 30g of pine nuts
- 30g of raisins
- 2 tablespoons of olive oil
- Salt q.b.

Preparation

1. Preparing the spinach: Clean the spinach by removing the hardest stems. Rinse well under cold running water.
2. Preparation of raisins and pine nuts: Put the raisins in a bowl with hot water and let it soften for about 10 minutes. Meanwhile, toast the pine nuts in a non-stick frying pan without oil for about 2-3 minutes, or until golden brown.
3. Cooking the spinach: Heat the olive oil in a large pan. Add the spinach and a pinch of salt. Cook them for 5-7 minutes, or until they are wilted.
4. Complete the recipe: Drain the raisins and add them to the spinach along with the toasted pine nuts. Mix well and cook for another 2-3 minutes.
5. Preparation for transport: Transfer the spinach to an airtight container and refrigerate until lunch.

19. PIZZA WITH BUTTERNUT PUMPKIN, MUSHROOMS AND GOAT CHEESE

Preparation time: 20 min
Cooking time: 15 min

Calories: 350 kcal
Fats: 15 g
Fibres: 4 g
Protein: 10 g
Carbohydrates: 45 g
Sugars: 3 g

Ingredients

- 1 base for pizza
- 200g of pumpkin Butternut
- 100g of mushroom mushrooms
- 100g of goat cheese
- 2 tablespoons of olive oil
- Salt and pepper q.b.

Preparation

1. Preparation of the pumpkin: Peel and cut the pumpkin Butternut into small pieces. Put in a bowl, add a tablespoon of olive oil, salt and pepper. Mix to evenly distribute the seasoning.
2. Cooking the pumpkin: Place the pumpkin on a baking sheet and bake in a pre-heated oven at 200 ºC for about 15 minutes, or until it is tender.
3. Preparation of mushrooms: Clean the mushrooms with a damp cloth and cut into slices. Heat a tablespoon of olive oil in a pan and cook the mushrooms until golden brown.
4. Pizza assembly: Roll out the pizza base on a baking sheet. Spread the pumpkin, mushrooms and goat cheese evenly on the base. Bake at 200 ºC for 10-15 minutes, or until the crust is golden brown and the cheese melted.
5. Preparation for transport: Allow the pizza to cool, then cut it into slices and transfer it to an airtight container. Store in the fridge until lunch.

NOTE 19 (pg 132)

20. SWEET CURRY POTATOES WITH WALNUTS AND FRESH CORIANDER

Preparation time: 15min
Cooking time: 30min

Calories: 350kcal   Protein: 6g
Fats: 20g   Carbohydrates: 30g
Fibres: 6g   Sugars: 10g

Ingredients

- 2 sweet potatoes of medium size
- 2 teaspoons curry powder
- 2 tablespoons of olive oil
- Salt q.b.
- 50g of nuts
- Fresh coriander q.b.

Preparation

1. Preparation of Sweet Potatoes: Wash and peel the sweet potatoes, then cut them into cubes of similar size to ensure uniform cooking.
2. Baking Sweet Potatoes: Arrange the sweet potato cubes on a baking sheet lined with baking paper, season with olive oil, curry powder and a pinch of salt. Mix well to make the ingredients stick. Bake at 200 ºC for about 30 minutes, or until the potatoes are tender and golden brown.
3. Preparation of the Nuts: Meanwhile, roughly chop the nuts.
4. Assembly of the Schiscetta: When the sweet potatoes are ready, let them cool slightly before adding the chopped nuts and fresh coriander. Mix gently to combine.
5. Preparation for Transport: Transfer the curry sweet potatoes with walnuts and coriander into an airtight container and refrigerate until lunch.

21. MIXED MUSHROOM OMELET WITH CARAMELIZED ONIONS

Preparation time: 15 min
Cooking time: 20 min

Calories: 300 kcal   Protein: 15 g
Fats: 15 g   Carbohydrates: 10 g
Fibres: 2 g   Sugars: 4 g

Ingredients

- 200g of mixed mushrooms
- 2 medium onions
- 4 eggs
- 2 tablespoons of olive oil
- Salt and pepper q.b.

Preparation

1. Preparation of Mushrooms and Onions: Clean the mushrooms with a damp cloth and slice them. Peel and slice the onions.
2. Cooking Mushrooms and Onions: In a non-stick pan, heat the olive oil and add the onions, cook over medium-low heat until they become golden and caramelized, about 10 minutes. Add the mushrooms and cook until they become golden brown, about 5-7 minutes.
3. Preparation of the Omelette: In a bowl, beat the eggs and season with salt and pepper. Pour the beaten eggs into the pan on the mushrooms and onions, cook over low heat until the omelet is no longer liquid, about 5-7 minutes.
4. Assembly of the Schiscetta: Allow the omelette to cool before transferring it into an airtight container.
5. Preparation for Transport: Keep the omelette in the fridge until lunch.

Preparation time: 15 min
Cooking time: 0 min

Calories: 300 kcal   Protein: 12 g
Fats: 15 g   Carbohydrates: 25 g
Fibres: 5 g   Sugars: 15 g

Ingredients

- 2 ripe pears
- 100g of gorgonzola cheese
- 50g of nuts
- 100g of arugula
- 2 tablespoons of balsamic vinegar
- Olive oil, salt and pepper q.b.

Preparation

1. Preparing pears: Cut the pears into thin slices by removing the core.
2. Preparation of nuts: Break the nuts and separate the kernels.
3. Preparation of gorgonzola: Cut the gorgonzola into cubes.
4. Salad assembly: Place a layer of arugula in a large dish. Add the pear slices and the gorgonzola cubes. Sprinkle over the walnut kernels.
5. Seasoning: Season with olive oil, balsamic vinegar, salt and pepper to taste.
6. Preparation for transport: Transfer the salad to an airtight container and keep in the fridge until lunch.

23. BRIE CHEESE AND GRAPE TART WITH HONEY AND NUTS

Preparation time: 20 min
Cooking time: 25 min

Calories: 350 kcal
Fats: 15 g
Fibres: 2 g
Protein: 10 g
Carbohydrates: 40 g
Sugars: 20 g

Ingredients

- 1 roll of puff pastry
- 200g of Brie cheese
- 300g of sweet white grapes
- 50g of nuts
- 2 tablespoons of honey
- Olive oil, salt q.b.

Preparation

1. Puff pastry preparation: Unroll the puff pastry on a baking sheet lined with baking paper. Preheat the oven to 180 °C.
2. Preparation of grapes and Brie: Cut the grapes in half by removing the seeds if present. Cut the Brie into thin slices.
3. Assembly of the tart: Arrange the slices of Brie on the puff pastry, then distribute the grapes and nuts.
4. Baking the tart: Bake in a preheated oven at 180 °C for about 20-25 minutes or until the puff pastry is golden and crispy.
5. Finish: Once cooled, season the tart with honey.
6. Preparation for transport: Transfer the tart to an airtight container and keep in the fridge until lunch.

BAKED FIGS WITH CRISPY BACON AND FIG JAM

Preparation time: 15 min
Cooking time: 15 min

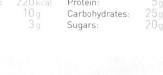

Calories:	220 kcal	Protein:	5 g
Fats:	10 g	Carbohydrates:	25 g
Fibres:	3 g	Sugars:	20 g

Ingredients

- 8 fresh figs
- 16 thin slices of bacon
- 4 tablespoons of fig jam
- Salt and pepper q.b.

Preparation

1. Preparation of figs: Wash the figs, cut them in half and sprinkle with a pinch of salt and pepper.
2. Wrapping the figs: Wrap each half of the fig with a slice of bacon.
3. Baking figs: Place the figs wrapped in a baking sheet lined with baking paper. Bake in the preheated oven at 180 ºC for 15 minutes or until the bacon is crispy.
4. Serve the figs: Once cooked, remove the figs from the oven and arrange them on a plate. Complete with a tablespoon of fig jam on each.
5. Preparation for transport: Transfer the figs in an airtight container and keep in the fridge until lunch.

25. RISOTTO WITH CHESTNUTS AND SAUSAGE

Preparation time: 10 min
Cooking time: 30 min

Calories: 400 kcal
Fats: 15 g
Fibres: 3 g
Protein: 10 g
Carbohydrates: 50 g
Sugars: 2 g

Ingredients

- 200g of rice for risotto
- 100g of peeled chestnuts
- 100g of sausage
- 1/2 glass of white wine
- 1/2 onion
- Broth q.b.
- 30g of butter
- Salt and pepper q.b.

Preparation

1. Cooking chestnuts: Put the chestnuts in a pot with water and cook until they become soft. Drain and set aside.
2. Preparation of the sauté: In a large pan, melt the butter and add the finely chopped onion. Fry until it becomes transparent.
3. Adding rice and sausage: Add the rice and crumbled sausage to the pan. Stir well and sauté for a few minutes, then add the white wine.
4. Cooking the risotto: Gradually add the hot broth and continue stirring until the rice is al dente.
5. Finish the risotto: Add the chestnuts, salt and pepper rule and mix well.
6. Preparation for transport: Transfer the risotto to an airtight container and keep in the fridge until lunch.

WINTER

01. LENTIL AND VEGETABLE SOUP

Preparation time: 15 min
Cooking time: 30 min

Calories: 300 kcal
Fats: 5 g
Fibres: 10 g
Protein: 15 g
Carbohydrates: 50 g
Sugars: 8 g

Ingredients

- 200 grams of dried lentils
- 2 carrots
- 2 ribs of celery
- 1 onion
- 2 potatoes
- 1 liter of vegetable broth
- Salt and pepper q.b.
- Extra virgin olive oil
- 1 bay leaf

Preparation

1. Preparation of lentils: Start by soaking the dried lentils in cold water for at least 2 hours. If you use pre-cooked lentils, you can skip this step.
2. Preparation of vegetables: Clean and finely chop the onion, carrots and celery ribs. Peel the potatoes and cut into cubes.
3. Cooking the vegetables: In a large pot, heat a little oil and add the chopped onion. Cook until transparent, then add carrots and celery. Cook over medium heat for about 5 minutes, until the vegetables begin to soften.
4. Cooking the lentils: Drain the lentils and add them to the pot together with the potatoes and the bay leaf. Stir to add flavour, then pour in the vegetable stock. Bring to a boil, then reduce the heat and cook covered for about 30-40 minutes, until the lentils and potatoes are tender.
5. Seasoning adjustment: Taste the soup and season with salt and pepper to your taste.
6. Preparation for transport: Once the soup has cooled, place it in an airtight container. If you have a thermos, you can use it to keep the soup warm until lunch.

NOTE 1 (pg 134)

POLENTA WITH MUSHROOM RAGOUT

Preparation time:	15 min		
Cooking time:	35 min		

Calories:	400 kcal	Protein:	10 g
Fats:	10 g	Carbohydrates:	60 g
Fibres:	8 g	Sugars:	5 g

Ingredients

- 250 gr of instant polenta
- 500 grams of mixed mushrooms
- 1 onion
- 2 cloves of garlic
- 1 glass of red wine
- Extra virgin olive oil
- Salt and pepper q.b.

Preparation

1. Preparation of the mushroom ragout: Clean the mushrooms with a damp cloth and cut into slices. In a large pan, fry the chopped onion and garlic in a little oil. Add the mushrooms and cook until they release their juices. Pour the red wine and let it evaporate. Finally, rule salt and pepper.
2. Polenta preparation: While the meat sauce is cooking, prepare the polenta according to the instructions on the package. Usually, you pour the polenta in salted boiling water, stirring constantly to avoid lumps. Once cooked, turn off the heat and cover.
3. Dish assembly: Once the polenta and meat sauce are ready, serve the polenta in a bowl and cover with the mushroom sauce.
4. Preparation for transport: Once the dish has cooled, transfer it to an airtight container. You can microwave it or enjoy it at room temperature

03. SPINACH AND RICOTTA QUICHE

Preparation time: 20 min
Cooking time: 40 min

Calories: 300 kcal
Fats: 20 g
Fibres: 3 g
Protein: 12 g
Carbohydrates: 20 g
Sugars: 2 g

Ingredients

- 1 roll of brisée pastry
- 400 grams of spinach
- 200 grams of ricotta cheese
- 2 eggs
- Salt and pepper q.b.

Preparation

1. Preparing the spinach: Clean the spinach and cook in a pan with a little oil until they wilt. Let them cool and squeeze to remove excess water.
2. Preparation of the filling: In a bowl, mix the ricotta with eggs, salt and pepper rule. Add the spinach and stir until smooth.
3. Quiche assembly: Spread the pastry in a quiche pan and prick the bottom with a fork. Pour the spinach and ricotta filling over the pasta.
4. Quiche cooking: Bake quiche in preheated oven at 180 °C for 30-35 minutes or until the surface is golden brown.
5. Preparation for transport: Once cooled, cut the quiche into portions and transfer them to an airtight container. You can enjoy it cold or microwave.

NOTE 3 (pg 134)

RISOTTO WITH LEEKS AND TALEGGIO

Preparation time: 10 min
Cooking time: 20 min

Calories: 500 kcal   Protein: 15 g
Fats: 15 g   Carbohydrates: 70 g
Fibres: 3 g   Sugars: 2 g

Ingredients

- 200 grams of carna-roli rice
- 2 leeks
- 100 grams of taleggio
- 1 liter of vegetable broth
- Extra virgin olive oil
- Salt and pepper q.b.

Preparation

1. Risotto preparation: Clean the leeks and cut them into thin slices. In a large pot, fry the leeks in a little oil until they become transparent. Add the rice and toast for a couple of minutes. Start adding the vegetable stock, one ladle at a time, stirring constantly.
2. Cooking the risotto: Continue to cook the risotto, adding broth every time it dries, for about 15-18 minutes or until the rice is al dente.
3. Assembly of the dish: Once the rice is al dente, add the taleggio into small pieces and stir until it is completely dissolved. Salt and pepper rule.
4. Preparation for transport: Let the risotto cool and transfer it to an airtight container. You can microwave it or enjoy it at room temperature.

05. QUINOA WITH PUMPKIN AND SPINACH

Preparation time:	15 min	Calories:	400 kcal	Protein:	12 g
Cooking time:	20 min	Fats:	15 g	Carbohydrates:	50 g
		Fibres:	8 g	Sugars:	5 g

Ingredients

- 200 grams of quinoa
- 300 grams of pumpkin
- 200 grams of fresh spinach
- 1 onion
- 2 cloves of garlic
- Extra virgin olive oil
- Salt and pepper q.b.
- Vegetable broth

Preparation

1. Preparation of quinoa: Rinse quinoa under running water to remove saponin, a natural compound that can give a bitter taste. Cook the quinoa in salted boiling water or vegetable broth for 15 minutes, then drain and set aside.

2. Preparation of the pumpkin: Meanwhile, clean the pumpkin, remove the peel and seeds and cut into cubes. In a large pan, fry the chopped onion and garlic in a little oil until transparent. Add the pumpkin and cook over medium heat for 10-15 minutes, until the pumpkin is soft. If necessary, add some vegetable stock to prevent the pumpkin from sticking.

3. Add spinach: Add the washed spinach and cook until it has wilted. Add the cooked quinoa, mix well and salt and pepper rule.

4. Preparation for transport: Let the quinoa cool with pumpkin and spinach and place it in an airtight container. You can enjoy it cold or microwave.

NOTE 5 (pg 134)

06. BLACK CABBAGE AND RICOTTA OMELET

Preparation time: 15min
Cooking time: 10min

Calories: 250kcal   Protein: 12g
Fats: 15g   Carbohydrates: 10g
Fibres: 3g   Sugars: 2g

Ingredients

- 4 eggs
- 200 grams of kale
- 100 grams of ricotta cheese
- Salt and pepper q.b.
- Extra virgin olive oil

Preparation

1. Preparation of the cabbage: Clean the kale, remove the central coast and cut the leaves into strips. In a large pan, fry the kale in a little oil until it has wilted.
2. Preparing the omelet: In a bowl, beat the eggs with the ricotta, salt and pepper. Add the kale and mix well. In a non-stick frying pan, cook the omelet over medium heat for 5-7 minutes per side, until it is golden brown.
3. Preparation for transport: Let the omelette cool and cut it into wedges. Transfer the slices into an airtight container. You can enjoy cold omelet or microwave.

07. BEETROOT, FETA AND WALNUT SALAD

| Preparation time: | 15 min |
| Cooking time: | 30 min |

Calories:	250 kcal	Protein:	8 g
Fats:	15 g	Carbohydrates:	20 g
Fibres:	5 g	Sugars:	15 g

Ingredients

- 4 beets
- 100 grams of feta
- 50 grams of nuts
- Extra virgin olive oil
- Balsamic vinegar
- Salt and pepper q.b.

Preparation

1. Preparation of beets: Cook the beets in boiling water until tender, then let them cool, Pelale and cut into cubes.
2. Preparation of the salad: In a bowl, mix the beets with the crumbled feta and the roughly chopped walnuts. Season with oil, balsamic vinegar, salt and pepper.
3. Preparation for transport: Transfer the salad to an airtight container. You can enjoy it cold or at room temperature.

NOTE 7 (pg 134)

08. CHICKEN ROLLS WITH SPINACH AND MOZZARELLA

Preparation time: 20 min
Cooking time: 20 min

Calories: 350 kcal
Fats: 15 g
Fibres: 2 g
Protein: 40 g
Carbohydrates: 5 g
Sugars: 2 g

Ingredients

- 4 breasts of chicken
- 200 grams of fresh spinach
- 200 grams of mozzarella
- 4 slices of cooked ham
- Extra virgin olive oil
- Salt and pepper q.b.

Preparation

1. Prepare the spinach: Clean the spinach and boil it in boiling water for a few minutes, until it wilts. Drain and squeeze well to remove excess water.
2. Preparation of the rolls: Flatten the chicken breasts with a meat tenderizer until you get a uniform thickness. Salt and pepper lightly. Place a slice of ham, spinach and some mozzarella on each chicken breast. Roll the chicken breast into a roll and set with toothpicks to prevent it from opening during cooking.
3. Cooking the rolls: In a non-stick pan, heat a little oil and brown the rolls on all sides until golden brown. Cover the pan and cook over medium heat for about 20 minutes, turning the rolls occasionally.
4. Preparation for transport: Let the rolls cool and cut into slices. Transfer the slices into an airtight container. You can enjoy cold or microwave-heated rolls.

09. BAKED PASTA WITH BROCCOLI AND SAUSAGE

Preparation time:	20 min		
Cooking time:	30 min		

Calories:	500 kcal	Protein:	25 g
Fats:	20 g	Carbohydrates:	50 g
Fibres:	5 g	Sugars:	5 g

Ingredients

- 250 g short pasta (e.g. penne)
- 1 broccoli
- 2 sausages
- 200 grams of mozzarella
- 50 grams of grated parmesan cheese
- Extra virgin olive oil
- Salt and pepper q.b.

Preparation

1. Preparation of broccoli: Clean the broccoli, divide the flowers and boil them in salted boiling water for 5 minutes. Drain and set aside.
2. Preparation of the sausage: In a non-stick pan, heat a little oil and brown the crumbled sausage until golden brown.
3. Preparation of the pasta: Cook the pasta in salted boiling water according to the instructions on the package, but drain a couple of minutes before the indicated cooking time.
4. Assembly and baking of the baked pasta: In a bowl, combine the pasta, broccoli, sausage, mozzarella cubes and half the parmesan. Mix well and transfer the mixture to an oven dish. Sprinkle with the remaining Parmesan cheese and bake at 200ºC for 20 minutes, or until the surface is golden.
5. Preparation for transport: Let the dough cool in the oven and transfer it to an airtight container. You can enjoy it cold or microwave.

NOTE 9 (pg 134)

10. CHICKPEA SOUP AND BLACK CABBAGE

Preparation time: 15min
Cooking time: 25min

Calories: 300kcal Protein: 15g
Fats: 5g Carbohydrates: 50g
Fibres: 10g Sugars: 5g

Ingredients

- 200 grams of dried chickpeas (or 400 grams of canned chickpeas)
- 200 grams of kale
- 1 onion
- 2 cloves of garlic
- 1 carrot
- 1 side of celery
- Extra virgin olive oil
- Salt and pepper q.b.

Preparation

1. Preparation of chickpeas: If you use dry chickpeas, soak them in cold water for at least 12 hours. Drain and rinse the chickpeas, then cook in boiling water for 1-2 hours, or until tender.
2. Preparation of the soup: In a large pot, fry the onion, garlic, carrot and celery chopped in a little oil. Add the clean, sliced kale and cook over medium heat for 10 minutes. Add the chickpeas and cover with water. Cook over medium heat for 30 minutes. Salt and pepper rule.
3. Preparation for transport: Let the soup cool and transfer it to an airtight container. You can enjoy it cold or microwave-heated.

NOTE 10 (pg 134)

11. RISOTTO WITH PUMPKIN AND GORGONZOLA

Preparation time: 10 min
Cooking time: 20 min

Calories: 450 kcal   Protein: 10 g
Fats: 10 g   Carbohydrates: 80 g
Fibres: 5 g   Sugars: 5 g

Ingredients

- 200 grams of carna-roli rice
- 300 grams of pumpkin
- 100 grams of gorgonzola cheese
- 1 onion
- 1 liter of vegetable broth
- Extra virgin olive oil
- Salt and pepper q.b.

Preparation

1. Preparation of the pumpkin: Clean the pumpkin by removing the peel and seeds, then cut into cubes.
2. Preparation of the risotto: In a large pan, heat a little oil and fry the chopped onion until it becomes transparent. Add the pumpkin and cook for 5 minutes. Add the rice and toast for a few minutes while stirring constantly.
3. Cooking risotto: Add the broth little by little, waiting for the rice to absorb the broth before adding more. Keep this up until the rice is cooked, it'll take about 18 minutes. At the end of cooking, add the chopped gorgonzola and mix well until it has dissolved. Salt and pepper rule.
4. Preparation for transport: Let the risotto cool and transfer it to an airtight container. You can enjoy it cold or microwave-heated.

12. POLENTA WITH MUSHROOMS AND TALEGGIO

Preparation time: 15 min
Cooking time: 30 min

Calories: 500 kcal   Protein: 15 g
Fats: 20 g   Carbohydrates: 60 g
Fibres: 5 g   Sugars: 3 g

Ingredients

- 200 grams of corn flour for polenta
- 300 grams of mixed mushrooms
- 200 grams of taleggio
- 1 clove of garlic
- Extra virgin olive oil
- Salt and pepper q.b.

Preparation

1. Preparation of the polenta: In a large pot, bring to a boil 1 liter of salted water. Pour in the cornmeal and stir continuously to avoid lumps. Let it simmer for about 40 minutes, stirring occasionally.
2. Preparation of mushrooms: In a pan, heat a little oil and fry the whole garlic clove. Add the cleaned and chopped mushrooms and cook over medium heat for 10 minutes. Salt and pepper rule.
3. Assembly of the dish: Cut the taleggio into pieces and Mescolalo polenta still hot until it is dissolved. Add the mushrooms and mix well.
4. Preparation for transport: Let the polenta cool with mushrooms and taleggio and transfer it to an airtight container. You can enjoy it cold or microwave.

13. BARLEY WITH VEGETABLES AND SAUSAGE

Preparation time:	20 min	Calories:	400 kcal	Protein:	15 g
Cooking time:	25 min	Fats:	15 g	Carbohydrates:	50 g
		Fibres:	5 g	Sugars:	3 g

Ingredients

- 200 grams of barley
- 2 sausages
- 1 zucchini
- 1 carrot
- 1 bell pepper
- Extra virgin olive oil
- Salt and pepper q.b.

Preparation

1. Preparation of barley: Soak the barley in cold water for at least 2 hours. Then rinse well under running water and drain.
2. Preparation of vegetables and sausage: Clean all vegetables and cut into cubes. Remove the skin from the sausages and crumble.
3. Cooking barley, vegetables and sausage: In a large pan, heat a little oil and fry the vegetables for 5 minutes. Add the crumbled sausage and barley, mix well and cook for another 10 minutes, adding water if necessary. Salt and pepper rule.
4. Preparation for transport: Let the dish cool and transfer it to an airtight container. You can enjoy it cold or microwave-heated.

NOTE 13 (pg 134)

14. PASTA E CECI

Preparation time: 10 min
Cooking time: 20 min

Calories: 400 kcal   Protein: 15 g
Fats: 5 g   Carbohydrates: 70 g
Fibres: 10 g   Sugars: 3 g

Ingredients

- 200 grams of pasta
- 200 grams of dried chickpeas
- 1 onion
- 2 cloves of garlic
- 1 sprig of rosemary
- 1 liter of vegetable broth
- Extra virgin olive oil
- Salt and pepper q.b.

Preparation

1. Preparing the chickpeas: Soak the chickpeas in cold water for at least 12 hours. After this time, rinse well under running water and drain.
2. Preparation of the pasta and chickpeas: In a large pot, heat a little oil and fry the chopped onion and garlic until they become transparent. Add the chickpeas and rosemary and cover with the vegetable stock. Bring to a boil, then lower the heat and simmer for about 1 hour, or until the chickpeas are tender.
3. Pasta cooking: When the chickpeas are almost ready, add the pasta and cook for the time indicated on the package. If necessary, add more broth or water. Salt and pepper rule.
4. Preparation for transport: Let the pasta and chickpeas cool and transfer it to an airtight container. You can enjoy it cold or microwave.

15. WILD RICE WITH WINTER VEGETABLES

Preparation time: 10 min
Cooking time: 40 min

Calories: 330 kcal
Fats: 5 g
Fibres: 5 g
Protein: 7 g
Carbohydrates: 63 g
Sugars: 5 g

Ingredients

- 200 grams of wild rice
- 1/2 red cabbage
- 2 turnips
- 1 onion
- 2 cloves of garlic
- 1 liter of vegetable broth
- Extra virgin olive oil
- Salt and pepper q.b.

Preparation

1. Preparation of the vegetables: Clean the pumpkin by removing the seeds and peel, then cut into cubes. Also clean the carrots and cut into slices. Finally, chop the onion and garlic.
2. Cooking rice: In a large pot, heat a little oil and fry the onion and garlic until transparent. Add the wild rice and toast for a couple of minutes, stirring frequently.
3. Adding vegetables: Combine the vegetables with the rice and mix well. Then, cover everything with the vegetable broth and cook over medium heat for about 40 minutes, or until the rice is cooked and has absorbed almost all the broth. Salt and pepper rule.
4. Preparation for transport: Let the rice cool with the vegetables and transfer it to an airtight container. You can enjoy it cold or microwave-heated.

NOTE 15 (pg 134)

16. CHICKEN WITH BAKED POTATOES

Preparation time: 15 min
Cooking time: 40 min

Calories: 450 kcal Protein: 30 g
Fats: 20 g Carbohydrates: 35 g
Fibres: 5 g Sugars: 2 g

Ingredients

- 2 chicken legs
- 4 medium potatoes
- Rosemary q.b.
- Extra virgin olive oil
- Salt and pepper q.b.

Preparation

1. Preparation of chicken and potatoes: Clean the chicken legs and put them in a bowl. Also clean the potatoes and cut them into wedges. Add them to the bowl with the chicken.
2. Marinating the chicken and potatoes: Add rosemary, a little oil, salt and pepper. Mix well so that the chicken and potatoes are well seasoned. Leave to marinate for at least 30 minutes.
3. Baking: Preheat the oven to 200 ºC. Transfer the chicken and potatoes to a baking tray lined with baking paper and cook for about 45 minutes, or until the chicken is golden brown and the potatoes are cooked.
4. Preparation for transport: Allow the chicken and potatoes to cool and transfer them to an airtight container. You can enjoy them cold or microwave.

NOTE 16 (pg 135)

17. LENTIL AND BARLEY SOUP

Preparation time: 15 min
Cooking time: 25 min

Calories:	250 kcal	Protein:	10 g
Fats:	5 g	Carbohydrates:	40 g
Fibres:	10 g	Sugars:	5 g

Ingredients

- 200 grams of dried lentils
- 100 grams of barley
- 2 carrots
- 2 ribs of celery
- 1 onion
- 1 liter of vegetable broth
- Extra virgin olive oil
- Salt and pepper q.b.

Preparation

1. Preparation of lentils and barley: Soak the lentils and barley in cold water for at least 2 hours. After this time, rinse well under running water and drain.
2. Preparation of the soup: In a large pot, heat a little oil and fry the chopped onion until it becomes transparent. Add the chopped carrots and celery. Mix well and cook for 5 minutes.
3. Cooking lentils and barley: Add lentils and barley and cover with vegetable stock. Bring to a boil, then lower the heat and simmer for about 40 minutes, or until the lentils and barley are tender. Salt and pepper rule.
4. Preparation for transport: Let the soup cool and transfer it to an airtight container. You can enjoy it cold or microwave.

NOTE 17 (pg 135)

18. POTATO AND ONION OMELET MIX

Preparation time: 10 min
Cooking time: 12 min

Calories: 250 kcal Protein: 12 g
Fats: 15 g Carbohydrates: 20 g
Fibres: 3 g Sugars: 3 g

Ingredients

- 4 eggs
- 2 medium potatoes
- 1 large onion
- Olive oil q.b.
- Salt and pepper q.b.

Preparation

1. Preparation of potatoes and onions: Clean the potatoes and onions and cut them into thin slices. In a non-stick frying pan, heat a little olive oil and add the potatoes and onions. Cook over medium heat for about 15-20 minutes, stirring occasionally, until soft.
2. Preparation of the eggs: Meanwhile, in a bowl, break the eggs and beat them with a fork. Add salt and pepper to taste.
3. Cooking the omelet: Once the potatoes and onions are cooked, pour the beaten eggs over the pan. Reduce the heat to a minimum, cover the pan with a lid and cook the omelet for about 10 minutes, or until the egg is cooked.
4. Preparation for transport: Let the omelette cool, cut it into pieces and place it in an airtight container. You can enjoy it cold or microwave.

19. SOUP WITH BEANS AND BACON

Preparation time: 15 min
Cooking time: 25 min

Calories:	350 kcal	Protein:	20 g
Fats:	10 g	Carbohydrates:	40 g
Fibres:	10 g	Sugars:	3 g

Ingredients

- 400 grams of dried beans
- 100 grams of bacon
- 1 onion
- 1 liter of chicken broth
- Extra virgin olive oil
- Salt and pepper q.b.

Preparation

1. Preparation of beans: Soak the beans in cold water for at least 8 hours. After this time, rinse well under running water and drain.
2. Preparation of the soup: In a large pot, heat a little oil and fry the chopped onion until it becomes transparent. Add the bacon cut into small pieces and brown until golden brown.
3. Cooking the beans: Add the beans and cover with the chicken stock. Bring to a boil, then lower the heat and simmer for about 1 hour and 30 minutes, or until the beans are tender. Salt and pepper rule.
4. Preparation for transport: Let the soup cool and transfer it to an airtight container. You can enjoy it cold or microwave-heated.

NOTE 19 (pg 135)

20. MEATBALLS OF LENTILS

Preparation time: 20 min
Cooking time: 20 min

Calories: 250 kcal   Protein: 10 g
Fats: 6 g   Carbohydrates: 40 g
Fibres: 10 g   Sugars: 5 g

Ingredients

- 200 grams of dried lentils
- 1 carrot
- 1 onion
- 1 clove of garlic
- 1 egg
- 50 grams of breadcrumbs
- Salt and pepper q.b.
- Extra virgin olive oil

Preparation

1. Preparation of lentils: Soak the lentils in cold water for at least 8 hours. Rinse under running water and drain.
2. Cooking the lentils: In a pot, add the lentils, carrot and onion cut into small pieces, garlic and cover with water. Bring to a boil and cook over medium heat for about 1 hour, or until the lentils are soft. Add salt at the end of cooking and drain the lentils.
3. Prepare the meatballs: Blend the lentils until you get a puree. Add the egg, breadcrumbs, salt and pepper and stir until you get a homogeneous mixture. Shape the meatballs with your hands and place them on a baking sheet lined with baking paper.
4. Cooking the meatballs: Bake at 200°C for about 20 minutes, or until the meatballs are golden brown.

NOTE 20 [pg 135]

21. VEGETABLE SOUP

Preparation time: 15 min
Cooking time: 35 min

Calories:	150 kcal	Protein:	4 g
Fats:	3 g	Carbohydrates:	30 g
Fibres:	5 g	Sugars:	5 g

Ingredients

- 2 carrots
- 2 potatoes
- 1 zucchini
- 1 onion
- 2 ribs of celery
- 1 liter of vegetable broth
- Salt and pepper q.b.
- Extra virgin olive oil

Preparation

1. Preparation of the vegetables: Clean all the vegetables and cut them into small pieces.
2. Cooking the soup: In a large pot, heat a little oil and add the onion. Sauté until transparent, then add all the other vegetables and stir. Cover with the vegetable stock and bring to a boil.
3. Cooking vegetables: Cook over medium heat for about 30 minutes, or until the vegetables will not be tender. Salt and pepper rule.
4. Preparation for transport: Let the soup cool and transfer it to an airtight container. You can enjoy it cold or microwave.

22. BARLEY SOUP WITH BEANS AND BEANS

Preparation time:	15 min	Calories:	200 kcal	Protein:	8 g
Cooking time:	30 min	Fats:	3 g	Carbohydrates:	35 g
		Fibres:	8 g	Sugars:	5 g

Ingredients

- 150 grams of pearl barley
- 200 grams of dry beans
- 2 carrots
- 2 ribs of celery
- 1 onion
- 1 liter of vegetable broth
- Salt and pepper q.b.
- Extra virgin olive oil
- 1 bay leaf

Preparation

1. Preparation of beans: Soak the beans in cold water for at least 8 hours. Rinse under running water and drain.
2. Preparation of vegetables: Clean and finely chop carrots, celery and onion.
3. Cooking the soup: In a large pot, heat a little oil and add the onion, carrots and celery. Sauté for a couple of minutes, then add the barley and beans. Mix well and then cover with the vegetable stock. Add the bay leaf, cover the pot and cook over medium heat for about 1 hour and a half, or until the barley and beans are tender.
4. Finish the dish: At the end of cooking, remove the bay leaf, add salt and pepper and add a little olive oil.
5. Preparation for transport: Let the soup cool and transfer it to an airtight container. You can enjoy it cold or microwave-heated.

23. RISOTTO WITH PORCINI MUSHROOMS

Preparation time:	10 min
Cooking time:	20 min

Calories:	450 kcal	Protein:	10 g
Fats:	10 g	Carbohydrates:	80 g
Fibres:	5 g	Sugars:	2 g

Ingredients

- 300 grams of Carnaroli rice
- 200 grams of porcini mushrooms
- 1 onion
- 1 liter of vegetable broth
- Salt and pepper q.b.
- Extra virgin olive oil
- 50 grams of grated parmesan cheese

Preparation

1. Preparation of mushrooms: Clean the mushrooms with a damp cloth, cut them into slices and set them aside.
2. Preparation of the risotto: In a large pot, heat a little oil and add the finely chopped onion. Sauté for a couple of minutes, then add the rice and toast for a few minutes, stirring constantly. Add the mushrooms and stir.
3. Cooking risotto: Add the broth one ladle at a time, waiting for it to be absorbed before adding the next. Continue until the rice is cooked al dente.
4. Finish the dish: At the end of cooking, turn off the heat, add the grated Parmesan cheese, salt and pepper rule and mix well.
5. Preparation for transport: Let the risotto cool and transfer it to an airtight container. You can enjoy it cold or microwave.

NOTE 23 (pg 135)

24. SPELT AND LENTIL SOUP

Preparation time: 15 min
Cooking time: 30 min

Calories: 350 kcal   Protein: 15 g
Fats: 5 g   Carbohydrates: 60 g
Fibres: 10 g   Sugars: 5 g

Ingredients

- 150 grams of pearl spelt
- 200 grams of dried lentils
- 2 carrots
- 2 ribs of celery
- 1 onion
- 1 liter of vegetable broth
- Salt and pepper q.b.
- Extra virgin olive oil

Preparation

1. Preparation of lentils: Soak the lentils in cold water for at least 8 hours. Rinse under running water and drain.
2. Preparation of vegetables: Clean and finely chop carrots, celery and onion.
3. Cooking the soup: In a large pot, heat a little oil and add the onion, carrots and celery. Sauté for a couple of minutes, then add the spelt and lentils. Mix well and then cover with the vegetable stock. Cover the pot and cook over medium heat for about 1 hour, or until the spelt and lentils are tender.
4. Finish the dish: At the end of cooking, salt and pepper and add a little olive oil.
5. Preparation for transport: Let the soup cool and transfer it to an airtight container. You can enjoy it cold or microwave.

25. BULGUR SALAD, BRUSSELS SPROUTS AND NUTS

Preparation time: 15 min
Cooking time: 10 min

Calories: 400 kcal
Fats: 15 g
Fibres: 7 g
Protein: 15 g
Carbohydrates: 50 g
Sugars: 5 g

Ingredients

- 200 grams of bulgur
- 200 grams of Brussels sprouts
- 50 grams of nuts
- Extra virgin olive oil
- Salt and pepper q.b.
- Juice of 1 lemon

Preparation

1. Preparing the bulgur: Cook the bulgur according to the instructions on the package. Once ready, drain and let it cool.
2. Preparing the Brussels sprouts: Clean the sprouts by removing the hard outer leaves, cut them in half and steam them for about 15 minutes.
3. Preparation of the salad: In a large bowl, combine the cooked and cooled bulgur, Brussels sprouts, roughly chopped walnuts. Season with oil, salt, pepper and lemon juice.
4. Preparation for transport: Transfer the salad to an airtight container. You can enjoy it cold.

NOTE 25 (pg 135)

SPRING

1. The Farro, Asparagus and Peas Salad consists of spelt, asparagus, peas, pecorino cheese and olive oil. Spelt provides complex carbohydrates and fiber. Asparagus and peas contribute vitamin K, vitamin A, vitamin C, fiber and antioxidants. Pecorino romano is a source of protein and calcium, while olive oil provides monounsaturated fats beneficial for the heart.

2. Pasta Fredda with cherry tomatoes, rocket and ricotta is a balanced combination of carbohydrates, proteins and vegetables. Wholegrain pasta provides complex carbohydrates and fiber, while cherry tomatoes and arugula add vitamin C, vitamin A, vitamin K and antioxidants. Ricotta is a source of protein and calcium. Olive oil is a source of monounsaturated fats beneficial for the heart.

3. The Spring Omelette of Quinoa, Carrots and Zucchini is a balanced combination of proteins, carbohydrates and vegetables. Quinoa provides complete proteins and complex carbohydrates. Carrots and zucchini provide vitamin A, vitamin C, potassium and fiber. Eggs are an excellent source of protein and vitamin B12. Olive oil is a source of monounsaturated fats that benefit the heart.

4. Bulgur with Chickpeas, Cabbage and Pecorino is a balanced combination of protein, carbohydrates and vegetables. Bulgur provides complex carbohydrates and fiber. Chickpeas are an excellent source of protein and fiber. Cabbage provides vitamin C, vitamin K, fiber and antioxidants. Pecorino is a source of protein and calcium. Olive oil is a source of monounsaturated fats that benefit the heart.

5. Couscous with asparagus, cherry tomatoes and buffalo mozzarella provides a balanced combination of carbohydrates, proteins and vegetables. Couscous provides complex carbohydrates. Asparagus is a source of vitamin K, vitamin C and fiber. Cherry tomatoes offer vitamin C and antioxidants. Buffalo mozzarella is a source of protein and calcium. Olive oil provides heart-beneficial monounsaturated Fats.

6. Eggs are an excellent source of high quality protein, B vitamins, vitamin D, and selenium. Asparagus offers vitamins A, C, E, K, and folic acid and is known for its diuretic properties. Chives provide vitamins A and C, calcium and iron.

7. Artichokes are rich in fiber, vitamin C, folate and other antioxidants. Radishes provide vitamins C and B, as well as having a refreshing and diuretic effect. Spring onions offer a mix of nutritional benefits, including vitamins A, C and B, potassium and fiber.

8. Risotto with fresh peas and mint is a refreshing and nourishing dish. Rice provides complex carbohydrates and proteins. Peas are a source of protein, fiber, vitamin A, vitamin C, vitamin K and folic acid. Mint adds a refreshing touch and is known for its digestive properties. Parmigiano Reggiano is a source of protein, calcium and phosphorus.

9. Spaghetti provides complex carbohydrates. Strawberries are an excellent source of vitamin C, manganese, antioxidants and folic acid. Arugula provides vitamins A, C, K, and a pinch of pepper. Parmigiano Reggiano adds flavor and provides protein, calcium and phosphorus.

10. Spinach is rich in iron, calcium, vitamins A, C and K, and antioxidants. Feta provides calcium and protein. Eggs are an excellent source of high quality protein, B and D vitamins and essential minerals such as selenium and zinc. Cooking cream provides fats, mainly saturated.

11. Beets are rich in vitamins A, C, K and minerals such as iron and calcium. Broad beans provide protein, fiber, B vitamins, iron and magnesium. Agretti are a good source of vitamin C, iron and calcium. Olive oil is a source of monounsaturated fats that are beneficial for heart health.

12. Lettuce provides vitamins A, C, K and B6, as well as minerals such as iron and calcium. Red turnips are rich in fiber, vitamin C, magnesium and folate. Egg offers high quality protein and vitamin D. Parmesan is a source of calcium and protein. Breadcrumbs add complex carbohydrates to the recipe.

13. Whole wheat bread provides complex carbohydrates, fiber and B-vitamins. Cottage cheese is an excellent source of protein and calcium. Ramerino, or rosemary, is known for its antioxidant and anti-inflammatory properties and provides vitamins A, C and B6. Olive oil offers monounsaturated fats, beneficial for cardiovascular health.

14. Tuna is an excellent source of high quality protein, omega-3, B vitamins, selenium and phosphorus. Cherries are rich in vitamins A, C, E, potassium and contain powerful antioxidants called anthocyanins that help reduce inflammation. Red onion provides vitamin C, vitamin B6, iron and fiber and is known for its antioxidant and anti-inflammatory properties. Extra virgin olive oil is rich in monounsaturated fats, vitamin E and phenolic compounds, beneficial for cardiovascular health.

15. Tuna provides high quality protein and omega-3, which are beneficial for cardiovascular health. Cherries are rich in vitamins C, A, potassium and antioxidants. Rhubarb is a source of vitamin K, C and contains dietary fiber. Turnip tops offer vitamins A, C, K, and a good amount of calcium, iron and magnesium. Olive oil is a source of monounsaturated fats that are beneficial for heart health.

16. Artichokes are known to be a source of fiber, vitamin C, folic acid, and antioxidants. Courgettes contain vitamins A, C, and K and are low-calorie. Zucchini flowers, while mainly decorative, contain small amounts of vitamins and minerals. Eggs are an excellent source of protein, vitamin D, B6, B12 and minerals such as zinc, iron and copper. Puff pastry or brisée contains complex carbohydrates and a good dose of fat, mainly saturated.

17. Cressonella, or cress, is rich in vitamins A and C and has antioxidant properties. Beetroot provides fiber, folic acid, manganese, and potassium. Feta cheese is a source of calcium and protein. Olive oil contains monounsaturated fats that are beneficial for heart health.

18. Chicken is a source of lean protein, vitamins B, iron, and zinc. Puntarelle provide vitamins A and C, potassium, and fiber. Basil contains vitamin K, B vitamins, iron, calcium and antioxidants. Olive oil is a source of monounsaturated fats that are beneficial for heart health.

19. Eggs provide high quality proteins, vitamins A, D, E and B12, and minerals such as phosphorus and selenium. Broccoli is an excellent source of vitamin C, vitamin K, folate and fiber. Ailoli, thanks to garlic, offers antioxidants and can have anti-inflammatory properties. Olive oil is a source of monounsaturated fats that are beneficial for heart health.

20. Chicken is an excellent source of lean protein and provides important vitamins and minerals such as niacin, vitamin B6 and phosphorus. Artichokes are rich in fiber, vitamin C, folic acid and have antioxidant properties. Basil provides vitamin K, vitamin A and contains anti-inflammatory compounds and antioxidants. Olive oil is a source of monounsaturated fats that are beneficial for heart health.

21. Asparagus is a rich source of vitamins A, C, E, K, folic acid and is known for its diuretic properties. Raw ham provides high quality protein, but also a significant amount of sodium. Olive oil is a source of monounsaturated fats that are beneficial for heart health.

22. Broad beans are a source of protein, vitamins A, C, B1, B2, folic acid and minerals such as iron, potassium, phosphorus and magnesium. Chives provide vitamin K, vitamin C and vitamin A. Eggs contain high quality proteins, vitamins and essential minerals. Flour is a source of complex carbohydrates.

23. Peas are a source of protein, fiber, vitamins A, C, K, B1, B3, folic acid and minerals such as iron, manganese, phosphorus and magnesium. Ricotta is rich in calcium, phosphorus, protein and B vitamins. Eggs provide high-quality proteins, vitamins and essential minerals.

24. Strawberries are rich in vitamins C, manganese, folic acid and contain powerful antioxidants. Mint provides vitamin A, iron and manganese. Cucumber and red pepper are sources of vitamin K, vitamin C and antioxidants. Olive oil offers monounsaturated fats that are beneficial for cardiovascular health.

25. Chicken is an excellent source of lean protein and also provides B vitamins, phosphorus and niacin. Radishes contain vitamin C and antioxidant compounds. Oregano has antibacterial and anti-inflammatory properties. Olive oil provides beneficial monounsaturated fats.

SUMMER

1. Le Whole grain tortillas provide fiber and complex carbohydrates that are essential for energy and intestinal health. Sliced turkey breast is an excellent source of lean protein and contains B vitamins, important for the health of the nervous system and energy metabolism. Avocado is a unique fruit that provides a good amount of heart-healthy monounsaturated fats, vitamin K, vitamin E, vitamin C and B vitamins, as well as fiber. Lettuce provides vitamin A, vitamin K, and a variety of other essential nutrients in smaller amounts. Finally, lemon juice is a rich source of vitamin C, an antioxidant that helps protect cells from free radical damage and promotes skin health.

2. Quinoa provides high quality protein, complex carbohydrates and fiber, as well as minerals such as magnesium, phosphorus, manganese and iron. Red beans are an excellent source of plant protein, fiber and iron, and they also contain B vitamins, potassium and magnesium. Peppers, both yellow and red, are rich in vitamins A, C and B6, and provide a good deal of fiber. Lemon juice provides vitamin C and enhances flavor without adding sodium. Extra virgin olive oil provides heart-healthy monounsaturated fats and vitamin E. Finally, fresh parsley is a source of vitamin K, vitamin C, vitamin A, folate and iron.

3. Whole-grain pens provide fiber and complex carbohydrates, beneficial for intestinal health and long-term energy. Cherry tomatoes are rich in vitamin C, potassium and contain lycopene, a powerful antioxidant. Natural tuna is an excellent source of lean protein and contains omega-3 fatty acids, B vitamins and minerals such as selenium. Arugula provides vitamin K, vitamin A, vitamin C and various antioxidant compounds. Finally, extra virgin olive oil provides healthy monounsaturated fats for the heart and vitamin E.

4. Basmati rice is a source of complex carbohydrates and contains B vitamins and various minerals such as magnesium and iron. Chicken breast provides lean protein, B vitamins and minerals such as selenium. Zucchini is rich in fiber, vitamin C and potassium, while carrot provides a significant amount of vitamin A, B vitamins and fiber. Red pepper is an excellent source of vitamin C and provides vitamin A, vitamin B6 and folic acid. Finally, extra virgin olive oil is rich in monounsaturated fats beneficial to heart health and vitamin E.

5. Wheat tortillas provide complex carbohydrates and a good amount of fiber. Hummus is a rich source of protein, fiber and healthy fats, thanks to chickpeas and sesame oil used to prepare it. Red pepper is an excellent source of vitamin C, vitamin A and folic acid. Carrot provides a large amount of vitamin A, B vitamins and fiber. Cucumbers are rich in water and provide vitamins such as vitamin K and vitamin C. Finally, fresh spinach leaves are rich in vitamin A, vitamin C, vitamin K, iron and calcium.

6. Stale bread provides complex carbohydrates and a fair amount of protein. Ripe tomatoes are an excellent source of vitamin C, vitamin K, potassium and antioxidants such as lycopene. The red onion offers a remarkable content of vitamin C, vitamin B6, fiber and antioxidants. Fresh basil is a source of vitamin K, vitamin A and antioxidants. Extra virgin olive oil is rich in monounsaturated fats, beneficial for cardiovascular health.

7. Wild rice is a source of high quality protein, fiber and minerals such as magnesium, phosphorus and manganese. Smoked salmon provides a significant dose of protein, omega-3 fatty acids, B vitamins and antioxidants such as astaxanthin. Cucumber contributes with vitamin K, vitamin C and a variety of antioxidants. Shallots offer a mix of B vitamins, vitamin C, fiber and antioxidants. Extra virgin olive oil is rich in monounsaturated fats, beneficial for cardiovascular health.

8. Cucumbers are rich in vitamin K, vitamin C and a variety of antioxidants. Greek yogurt is an excellent source of protein, calcium and probiotics beneficial to intestinal health. Garlic provides allicin, a sulfur compound known for its antimicrobial and cardioprotective properties. Lemon juice offers vitamin C and other antioxidants. Extra virgin olive oil is rich in monounsaturated fats, beneficial for cardiovascular health.

9. Quinoa is a gluten-free pseudo-cereal that provides high-quality protein, complex carbohydrates, fiber, and a variety of minerals such as magnesium, phosphorus, manganese, and iron. Tomatoes are rich in lycopene, a powerful antioxidant, vitamin C and vitamin K. Cucumber offers vitamins K and C, as well as a good amount of water for hydration. Spring onions provide vitamin C, vitamin A and various phytochemicals beneficial to health. Lemon juice is an excellent source of vitamin C and antioxidants. Extra virgin olive oil is rich in monounsaturated fats, beneficial for cardiovascular health. Mint and parsley are excellent sources of vitamin A, vitamin C, vitamin K and have antioxidant and anti-inflammatory properties.

10. Pasta is a source of complex carbohydrates that provide long-lasting energy. Feta, a Greek cheese, offers a good dose

of protein and calcium. Black olives are rich in monounsaturated and polyunsaturated fats, vitamin E and antioxidants. Cherry tomatoes provide vitamin C, vitamin K and the powerful antioxidant lycopene. The extra virgin olive oil, finally, is rich in monounsaturated fats beneficial for cardiovascular health.

11. Eggs are an excellent source of high-quality protein and vitamin B12. Zucchini is a source of B vitamins, vitamin C and fiber, as well as having a very low calorie content. Red peppers are rich in vitamin C, vitamin A and antioxidants such as beta-carotene. Onions provide a good dose of vitamin C, vitamin B6 and antioxidants, including quercetin. The extra virgin olive oil, finally, is rich in monounsaturated fats beneficial for cardiovascular health.

12. Grilled chicken breasts are a rich source of lean protein, B vitamins, especially B3 and B6, and minerals such as selenium. Romaine lettuce contributes vitamins A, C, K and folic acid. Cherry tomatoes are an excellent source of vitamin C and antioxidants such as lycopene. Cucumber, in addition to being moisturizing for its high water content, provides vitamins A and K. Feta is an excellent source of protein and calcium. Black olives are rich in monounsaturated fatty acids and vitamin E. Extra virgin olive oil, finally, is rich in monounsaturated fats beneficial for cardiovascular health.

13. Rice provides complex carbohydrates, a bit of protein and several B vitamins. Zucchini are rich in vitamins, including vitamin A, C and K, and minerals such as potassium and magnesium. Red pepper is known for its high content of vitamin C, vitamin A and antioxidants. Carrot is an excellent source of beta-carotene, which the body converts into vitamin A, and other vitamins such as vitamins K and B6. Canned tuna is a good source of high quality protein, B vitamins, especially niacin and B12, and minerals like selenium. Extra virgin olive oil, finally, is a rich source of monounsaturated fats beneficial to heart health.

14. Short pasta, preferably wholemeal, provides complex carbohydrates, fiber and a modest amount of protein. Arugula is notoriously rich in vitamins A and C, calcium and potassium. Almonds, rich in monounsaturated and polyunsaturated fats, provide fiber, protein, vitamin E and minerals such as magnesium and copper. Garlic is a remarkable source of manganese and vitamin B6 and has antimicrobial properties. Parmesan cheese is a rich source of protein and calcium. Extra virgin olive oil is a source of monounsaturated fats, beneficial for heart health.

15. Eggs are an excellent source of high biological value protein and provide vitamins A, D, E and B12, as well as minerals such as zinc and selenium. Fresh spinach is rich in vitamins A, C, K, folic acid and minerals such as iron, calcium and magnesium. Cottage cheese is a source of protein, calcium and vitamin B12, but also contains a moderate amount of saturated fat. Extra virgin olive oil provides monounsaturated fats beneficial to heart health and vitamin E.

16. Barley is a cereal rich in dietary fiber, protein, B vitamins and minerals such as magnesium, zinc and iron. Cherry tomatoes are a good source of vitamins A and C and provide a significant intake of lycopene, a powerful antioxidant. Pitted black olives are rich in monounsaturated fats, iron and vitamin E. Lemon juice is an excellent source of vitamin C and antioxidants. Extra virgin olive oil provides monounsaturated fats beneficial to heart health and vitamin E.

17. Chicken breast is an excellent source of lean protein and also provides B vitamins. Basmati rice, one of the lowest GI rice, is a good source of carbohydrates and provides fiber, B vitamins, and minerals such as magnesium and manganese. The teriyaki sauce, rich in flavor, contributes with sugar, salt and a minimum intake of vitamins and minerals. Sesame oil is rich in mono and polyunsaturated fats and vitamin E. Broccoli is a very nutritious vegetable, rich in vitamins A, C, K, folic acid, and fiber, as well as minerals such as calcium, potassium, and iron. Finally, sesame seeds added to garnish are a good source of fiber, protein, good fats, calcium, magnesium and phosphorus.

18. Quinoa, a gluten-free pseudo-cereal, provides high quality protein, complex carbohydrates and a good dose of fiber, as well as minerals such as magnesium, phosphorus, manganese and iron. Avocado is known for its healthy monounsaturated fats, fiber, vitamins such as vitamin K, C, E, B5, B6 and folate, and minerals such as potassium. Cherry tomatoes are rich in vitamin C and also contain vitamin A, potassium and fiber. Cucumber is known for its moisturizing properties, providing K and C vitamins and a number of minerals including potassium, magnesium, and manganese. Lemon juice is rich in vitamin C and contributes to the absorption of iron in the body. Finally, extra virgin olive oil is a source of monounsaturated fats beneficial to heart health.

19. Wholemeal bread is an excellent source of complex carbohydrates, fiber, and a number of vitamins and minerals including vitamin B, iron and magnesium. Tuna is an excellent source of lean protein, omega-3 fatty acids and vitamins such as B12 and niacin. Cucumber, mainly composed of water, offers vitamins K and C and a number of minerals including potassium, magnesium, and manganese. Light mayonnaise, although less nutritious than other ingredients, provides a certain amount of polyunsaturated and monounsaturated fats, which are beneficial for heart health.

20. Bulgur is a rich source of complex carbohydrates, fiber, protein and contains a number of vitamins and minerals, such

as vitamin B6, iron and magnesium. Ripe but firm tomatoes provide vitamin C, vitamin K, potassium and are known for their richness in lycopene, a powerful antioxidant. Parsley and fresh mint offer an abundance of vitamins A, C, K, iron and are known for their antioxidant and anti-inflammatory properties. Extra virgin olive oil is a source of monounsaturated fats beneficial to heart health. Lemon juice, in addition to giving flavor, adds a significant dose of vitamin C.

21. Black rice is a source of complex carbohydrates, fiber and protein, and contains unique antioxidants, known as anthocyanins. Shelled shrimps are an excellent source of protein, vitamin B12, phosphorus, iodine and selenium. Ripe mango offers a significant dose of vitamin C, vitamin A and contains various antioxidants. Lime juice, in addition to giving flavor, provides vitamin C. Extra virgin olive oil is a source of monounsaturated fats beneficial to heart health.

22. Whole wheat wraps provide dietary fiber and complex carbohydrates. Chicken breast is an excellent source of lean protein, vitamin B6 and niacin. Romaine lettuce offers vitamin A, vitamin K and folate. Grated parmesan is rich in calcium and protein. Caesar light sauce, although variable depending on the brand and recipe, can provide a lower dose of fat than the original version. Finally, extra virgin olive oil is a source of monounsaturated fats beneficial to heart health.

23. Salmon is an excellent source of high-quality protein, omega-3 fatty acids, and B vitamins. Quinoa, a gluten-free pseudo-cereal, provides high-quality protein, complex carbohydrates and a good dose of fiber, as well as minerals such as magnesium, phosphorus, manganese and iron. Asparagus is a rich source of vitamins A, C, E, K, folic acid and is known for its diuretic properties. Extra virgin olive oil is a source of monounsaturated fats beneficial to heart health.

24. Pasta provides complex carbohydrates, essential for daily energy, and a certain amount of protein. Cherry tomatoes are rich in vitamin C, potassium and lycopene, a powerful antioxidant. Pitted black olives are a source of healthy monounsaturated fats, iron and fiber. Salted cottage cheese provides high quality protein, calcium and vitamin B12. Extra virgin olive oil is a source of monounsaturated fats beneficial to heart health.

25. Wholemeal pasta provides a significant intake of fiber and complex carbohydrates, beneficial for intestinal health and for maintaining a sense of satiety prolonged. Red pepper is rich in vitamin C, vitamin B6, vitamin A and fiber. Zucchini provides B vitamins, vitamin C, potassium and fiber. Cherry tomatoes are a source of vitamin C, vitamin A, vitamin K and potassium. Feta, a typical Greek cheese, provides protein, calcium and vitamin B12. Olive oil is a source of monounsaturated fats beneficial to heart health and contains vitamin E and polyphenols, antioxidants that contribute to the protection of the body from oxidative stress. Finally, oregano, in addition to giving a touch of flavor, provides vitamins and minerals including vitamin K, iron and calcium.

AUTUMN

1. This delicious soup is rich in nutrients and flavor and is perfect to take to work as a light and healthy lunch. Butternut pumpkin is a valuable source of vitamin A, vitamin C and potassium, while carrots are rich in carotenoids, vitamin K and fiber. Garlic, in addition to giving the soup an irresistible aroma, has antibacterial properties. Garlic croutons, made with whole wheat bread, provide complex carbohydrates and fiber.

2. This tasty preparation is rich in vitamin A, potassium and fiber thanks to sweet potatoes. Rosemary gives a characteristic aroma and also has antioxidant properties. Nuts add proteins, monounsaturated and polyunsaturated fats, vitamins B and E and minerals such as magnesium and zinc.

3. Mushrooms are a good source of protein, fiber, B vitamins and mineral salts such as potassium. Creamy cheese provides calcium and protein, while parsley is rich in vitamin C and B vitamins.

4. Pears are a source of fiber, vitamin C, and beneficial antioxidants. Gorgonzola cheese offers an intense and creamy flavor, as well as providing protein and calcium. Honey brings natural sweetness and contains substances beneficial to health.

5. Grapes are a source of vitamins C, K and antioxidants. Nuts are rich in monounsaturated fats, proteins and omega-3 beneficial for the heart. Cheddar cheese provides protein and calcium. Honey brings natural sweetness and antibacterial properties.

6. Figs are rich in vitamins such as A, C, K and antioxidants. Raw ham is a source of protein and fat. Arugula provides vitamins A, C and K and minerals such as calcium and iron. Balsamic vinegar adds an aromatic touch without adding significant calories.

7. Cauliflower is a good source of vitamin C, vitamin K, folate and fiber. Hazelnuts provide monounsaturated fats, proteins and fiber, as well as vitamin E and magnesium. Sultanas are rich in natural carbohydrates and fiber. Lemon adds vitamin C and a fresh flavor to the dish.

8. Carrots are rich in vitamin A, vitamin K and potassium, contributing to the health of the eyes and the immune system. Honey adds natural sweetness and antioxidant properties, while ginger offers anti-inflammatory and digestive benefits.

9. Kale is rich in vitamins A, C and K, and offers an excellent source of fiber. Onions provide antioxidants and have anti-inflammatory properties. The base of the tart contains carbohydrates and fats, making it an indulgent choice for lunch.

10. Beets are rich in vitamin A, C and K, and offer a good amount of iron and calcium. Feta provides protein and calcium. Eggs provide high quality protein.

11. Kale is rich in vitamins A and C, and offers a good amount of fiber. Caramelized onions bring sweetness and flavor to the tart.

12. Brussels sprouts are rich in vitamins K, C, A and B6, as well as being a good source of fiber. Almonds contain protein, fiber, vitamin E and magnesium. Garlic is known for its antibacterial and anti-inflammatory properties.

13. Fennel is a source of fiber, vitamin C and potassium. Bechamel is a creamy dressing that provides protein and calcium, while Parmesan is a source of high quality protein and calcium.

14. Porcini mushrooms provide protein and fiber, along with B vitamins and minerals such as potassium and phosphorus. Rice is a slow-digesting carbohydrate source, while onions provide vitamin C, vitamin B6, fiber, and antioxidants.

15. Couscous provides slow-digesting carbohydrates and protein. Peppers are an excellent source of vitamins C and A, and provide fiber and antioxidants. Vegetables add essential fiber, vitamins and minerals to the diet.

16. Celery is rich in vitamin K, folic acid, fiber, potassium and vitamin C. Nuts are an excellent source of good fats, protein, fiber, vitamin E, B vitamins and minerals such as magnesium, iron, copper and zinc. Lemon is a rich source of vitamin C and flavonoids.

17. Turnips are rich in vitamin C, vitamin K, vitamin A, vitamin B6, folic acid and fiber. Rosemary is a source of antioxidants and rosmarinic acid. Garlic provides allicin, known for its antibacterial properties.

18. Spinach is rich in vitamins A, C, K, and minerals such as iron and calcium. Pine nuts are a source of protein, vitamin E, magnesium and zinc. Raisins provide fiber, iron, potassium and a variety of antioxidant polyphenols.

19. Butternut pumpkin is a source of vitamin A, vitamin C, potassium and fiber. Mushrooms provide proteins, B vitamins, antioxidants and minerals such as selenium. Goat cheese is rich in protein and calcium.

20. Sweet potatoes are an excellent source of vitamin A, vitamin C, fiber and potassium. Curry powder contains antioxidan-

ts and has anti-inflammatory properties. Nuts are rich in good fats, proteins, fiber, vitamins and minerals. Coriander has antioxidant, digestive and anti-inflammatory properties.

21. Mushrooms are a good source of protein, B vitamins, vitamin D, minerals and antioxidants. Caramelized onions provide natural sweetness and are rich in antioxidants. Eggs are an excellent source of high biological value protein and vitamins.

22. Pears provide vitamins C and K, as well as fiber and a natural sweetness. Nuts add crispness and are an excellent source of omega-3 polyunsaturated fats, vitamin E and vitamin B6. Gorgonzola, a blue cheese, provides protein and calcium. Arugula has a spicy taste and is rich in vitamins A and C, calcium and iron. Balsamic vinegar adds a sweet-sour taste. L'uva è una fonte di vitamine C e K, oltre a fornire un naturale dolcezza. Il Brie è un formaggio cremoso che fornisce proteine e calcio. Le noci sono una fonte eccellente di grassi polinsaturi omega-3, vitamina E e vitamina B6. Il miele aggiunge un sapore dolce e contiene antiossidanti. La pasta sfoglia fornisce carboidrati e un tocco croccante.

23. Figs are an excellent source of fiber, vitamins B6, C, K and minerals such as potassium, manganese and copper. Bacon provides protein and fat, but it is also a source of sodium. Fig jam, in addition to providing a sweet contrast to bacon, contains sugar.

24. Figs are a significant source of dietary fiber, B vitamins and minerals such as potassium. While bacon is a source of saturated fat, it also provides protein. Fig jam, in addition to providing a natural sweetness, preserves the fibers and vitamins of the fruit. Arborio rice used for risotto is rich in starch and provides a large dose of energy in the form of carbohydrates. Chestnuts are an excellent source of vitamin C, dietary fiber and potassium. Sausage provides proteins and fats, necessary for satiety.

WINTER

1. Le l Lentils mainly provide protein, fiber and complex carbohydrates. Vegetables (carrots, celery, onion, potatoes) contribute to vitamins, minerals and fiber.

2. Polenta mainly provides complex carbohydrates. Mushrooms, onion and garlic provide vitamins, minerals and fiber. Red wine contributes to flavor and could affect alcohol content (if any). Extra virgin olive oil affects the fat content. Salt and pepper contribute to the flavor.

3. Pasta brisée provides mainly carbohydrates and fats. Spinach and ricotta provide proteins, vitamins and minerals. Eggs contribute to the protein content. Salt and pepper contribute to the flavor.

4. Carnaroli rice provides mainly carbohydrates. Leeks and Taleggio provide proteins, fats and vitamins. Vegetable broth affects the sodium content. Salt and pepper contribute to the flavor.

5. Quinoa mainly provides proteins and carbohydrates. Pumpkin and spinach provide carbohydrates, fiber, vitamins and minerals. Onion and garlic affect the fiber content. Vegetable broth can contribute to the sodium content.

6. Eggs are a source of high-quality protein and also provide B vitamins. Kale provides vitamins A, C, and K, as well as minerals such as calcium and iron. Ricotta contributes with protein and calcium, while salt and pepper regulate the flavor. Extra virgin olive oil provides monounsaturated fats that are beneficial for heart health.

7. Beets provide B vitamins, vitamin C, and minerals such as iron and manganese. Feta provides protein and calcium, while nuts are rich in polyunsaturated fats, proteins, and minerals such as zinc and magnesium. The extra virgin olive oil contributes with monounsaturated fats beneficial to heart health. Balsamic vinegar, in addition to giving flavor, provides antioxidants.

8. Chicken breasts offer lean protein and are a source of B vitamins. Fresh spinach is rich in vitamins A, C, and K, as well as providing iron and calcium. Mozzarella contributes with protein and calcium. Cooked ham adds protein and fat. Extra virgin olive oil provides monounsaturated fats, beneficial for heart health.

9. Short pasta, a source of complex carbohydrates, provides energy with a gradual release. Broccoli adds vitamins A, C, and K, along with fiber and minerals such as potassium. Sausages provide protein, fat and sodium. Mozzarella, rich in protein and calcium, also helps to provide saturated fat. Grated parmesan offers protein, calcium and fat. Extra virgin olive oil provides monounsaturated fats, beneficial for heart health.

10. Chickpeas, a source of vegetable protein, complex carbohydrates and fiber, also provide iron, zinc and manganese. Kale, rich in vitamins A, C, and K, also offers folate and antioxidants. The onion and garlic cloves contribute sulfur compounds with a beneficial effect. Carrot and celery add vitamins and minerals, including potassium and vitamin C. Extra virgin olive oil provides monounsaturated fats, promoting heart health. Salt and pepper regulate the overall taste.

11. Carnaroli rice is a source of complex carbohydrates and provides gradual release energy. Pumpkin contributes with vitamins A, C, E, and K, as well as containing fiber, potassium and beta-carotene. Gorgonzola, a cheese rich in fat and protein, also provides calcium and phosphorus. Onion, in addition to giving flavor, contains antioxidants. Vegetable broth adds flavor without added fat. Extra virgin olive oil is a source of monounsaturated fats, beneficial for cardiovascular health. Salt and pepper regulate the overall taste.

12. Corn flour for polenta provides complex carbohydrates and is a source of energy, while mixed mushrooms contribute B vitamins, minerals such as potassium and proteins of plant origin. Taleggio, a cheese rich in fat and protein, also provides calcium and phosphorus. The garlic clove, in addition to conferring aroma, contains sulfur compounds with antioxidant properties. Extra virgin olive oil is rich in monounsaturated fats, beneficial for heart health. Salt and pepper regulate the flavor.

13. Barley is a source of complex carbohydrates and fiber, while sausages contribute to protein and fat. Vegetables add nutrients such as vitamins, minerals and fiber. Extra virgin olive oil provides healthy fats. Salt and pepper affect the flavor and sodium content.

14. Pasta provides complex carbohydrates, while chickpeas contribute to protein, fiber and carbohydrates. Onion and garlic add flavor and some nutrients. Extra virgin olive oil provides healthy fats.

15. Wild rice is a rich source of complex carbohydrates and fiber, contributing to a feeling of satiety and providing sustained energy. Winter vegetables such as pumpkin, carrots, onion and garlic are rich in vitamins, minerals and antioxidants beneficial to health. Extra virgin olive oil adds heart-healthy monounsaturated fats. The vegetable broth used as the basis of the preparation can provide various nutrients depending on the ingredients used. It is advisable to pay atten-

tion to the amounts of salt used, since the sodium content can vary depending on the broth and the salt added during cooking. The nutritional composition can be affected by portion sizes and variations in the preparation of ingredients.

16. Chicken thighs are a good source of high quality protein and also contain fat. Potatoes provide complex carbohydrates and a modest amount of fiber. Rosemary adds a characteristic aroma and flavor, but has a negligible nutritional impact in quantities used for cooking.

17. Lentils and barley are sources of plant protein and complex carbohydrates, which contribute to providing energy and nutrients. Carrots and celery add vitamins, minerals and fiber to the soup. Extra virgin olive oil provides healthy fats and contributes to the flavor of the dish. Salt and pepper affect the sodium content and taste. It is advisable to pay attention to the amounts of salt used, especially for those who must follow a low-sodium diet.

18. Potatoes and onions provide complex carbohydrates and fiber, while eggs provide high quality protein. Olive oil contributes to healthy fats and the flavor of omelette. Salt and pepper affect the sodium content and taste. It is advisable to pay attention to the amounts of salt used, especially for those who must follow a low-sodium diet. Nutritional values may vary depending on portion sizes and variations in ingredient preparation.

19. Beans are a good source of vegetable protein and fiber, while bacon provides protein and fat. Onion contributes to the flavor and provides some essential nutrients. Chicken broth can affect the sodium content of the soup. It is advisable to use soaked and cooked dried beans to reduce the preparation time. The bean and bacon soup is a hearty and nutritious dish, ideal for a warm and comforting meal during cold days.

20. Lentils are a good source of protein and fiber, ideal for a vegetarian or vegan diet. Carrot, onion and garlic clove provide essential vitamins and minerals. Egg and breadcrumbs are used as binders to form meatballs. Lentil meatballs can be cooked in the oven or in a pan with a little extra virgin olive oil, making them a healthier choice than traditional meatballs.

21. Vegetable soup is a healthy and nutritious dish, rich in vitamins and minerals. Carrots, potatoes, zucchini, onion and celery provide a variety of essential nutrients. Vegetable broth can be prepared using fresh vegetables or low-sodium canned broth. Extra virgin olive oil can be added to minestrone to enrich its flavor and bring healthy fats. Salt and pepper are used to season the dish.

22. Barley and bean soup is a hearty and nutritious recipe, ideal for colder days. Pearl barley provides complex carbohydrates and fiber, while borlotti beans provide protein and additional fiber intake. Carrots, celery and onion add a variety of vitamins and minerals, contributing to the goodness and completeness of the dish. Bay leaf is used to flavor the soup during cooking. Salt and pepper are used to season the dish to taste. Extra virgin olive oil can be added at the time of consumption to enrich the flavor and bring healthy fats.

23. Carnaroli rice is a variety of Italian rice with a high starch content, which contributes to its creamy texture during cooking. Porcini mushrooms are rich in proteins, vitamins B and minerals such as potassium and phosphorus. Onion adds flavor and contains fiber and vitamin C. Vegetable broth provides umami and aromas, but the nutritional values will depend on the ingredients used in the preparation of the broth. The extra virgin olive oil provides monounsaturated fats beneficial for the heart. Parmesan cheese contains proteins and fats, as well as calcium and vitamin D.

24. Spelt and lentil soup is a dish rich in vegetable proteins and fiber. Pearl spelt, a form of spelt with the shell removed, provides complex carbohydrates and a good amount of fiber. Lentils add protein, iron, and other important B vitamins. Carrots, celery ribs, and onions contribute to essential vitamins and minerals, as well as providing sweetness and flavor to the soup. Vegetable broth adds umami and aromas, but the nutritional values will depend on the ingredients used in its preparation. The extra virgin olive oil offers monounsaturated fats beneficial for the heart.

25. Bulgur provides complex carbohydrates and fiber from wholemeal pasta, which contribute to satiety and intestinal well-being. Brussels sprouts are a rich source of vitamin C, vitamin K and folate, while nuts add protein, beneficial polyunsaturated fats and vitamin E. Extra virgin olive oil offers heart-healthy monounsaturated fats, and lemon juice brings a note of freshness and vitamin C.

THANKS!

Printed in Great Britain
by Amazon

36718798R00077